# SQUEEZE PLAY

*Practical Insights for Men*
*Caught Between Work & Home*

# SQUEEZE PLAY

# BOB BRINER
**Author of *Roaring Lambs***

ZondervanPublishingHouse
*Grand Rapids, Michigan*

*A Division of HarperCollinsPublishers*

Requests for information should be addressed to:
Zondervan Publishing House
Grand Rapids, Michigan 49530

Briner, Bob.
    Squeeze play: practical insights for men caught between work &
home / Bob Briner.
        p. cm.
    ISBN: 0-310-40020-1 (hardcover)
    1. Businessmen—Religious life. 2. Christian life—1960–. I. Title.
BV4596.B8B69   1993
248.8'8–dc20                                                      93-8943
                                                                    CIP

Printed in the United States of America

*Edited by Lyn Cryderman*
*Cover illustration by Greg Tess*

94 95 96 97 98 99 /❖ DH / 10 9 8 7 6 5 4 3 2 1

*Dedicated to Dr. Robert E. Smith,*
*now president of Greenville College, who for*
*forty-five years as teammate, friend, and mentor*
*has helped me keep my eye on the prize.*

# Contents

# Acknowledgments

— —

As with *Roaring Lambs*, many people have contributed to *Squeeze Play*. Once again, my wonderful editor at Zondervan, Lyn Cryderman, contributed significantly to the quality of my writing. Publisher Scott Bolinder has been a great source of encouragement.

Without Sealy Yates, my astute literary agent, this book would never have happened. He has my thanks.

Dr. Ray Pritchard, senior pastor at Calvary Memorial Church in Oak Park, Illinois, once again helped with scriptural and theological questions. Any mistakes in this area are mine, not his.

Dennis Spencer, John Humphrey, my colleagues at ProServ, and my partner, Donald Dell, have been sources of encouragement and help. And my longtime faithful and efficient secretary, Mary Ann Milazzotto, typed the manuscript and aided in many other ways. To all of you, thanks.

# Introduction:
# Caught Between Third and Home

—•—

*Blessed is the man who by excellence of hand and speed of foot takes by strength and daring the highest of prizes.*

Pindar (the athlete's poet)

*Forgetting what is behind and straining toward what is ahead, I press on toward the goal to win the prize for which God has called me heavenward in Christ Jesus.*

Philippians 3:13–14

One of the most exciting plays in the game of baseball is that suspenseful interlude when a runner has gotten himself trapped between third and home. Anything can happen, even if both the runner and the encroaching fielders perform flawlessly. Until that runner is tagged out or makes it safely back to third or ahead to home, no one can predict the outcome. Talk about excitement! It's a high-tension moment in America's favorite pastime.

This back-and-forth race between runner and fielders goes by many names. When I was young, we used to call it getting in a hot box. You may have heard it referred to as a rundown. But the most exciting manifestation of this play is the squeeze play—a deliberate play whereby the runner is being "squeezed" home by a daring bunt laid down by his teammate. The runner on third base and the batter are each signaled that the play is on. As soon as the pitcher releases the ball, the runner takes off. In the meantime, the batter squares off and bunts. Ideally, the runner makes it in before a fielder can pick up the ball and throw it home, but, naturally, it doesn't always happen that way. Sometimes the ball is bunted too hard, allowing a fielder to throw the ball to the catcher well before the runner arrives. Worse, the bunt may pop up, allowing the defense to nail a sweet double play.

But if all goes right, the runner charges forward and slides under the tag to score, and when that happens the stadium erupts in wild appreciation. Even opponents admire the beauty and courage of the squeeze play—a play that pits the runner against the forces of chance and an aggressive defense.

I don't know about you, but as a follower of Christ and a globe-trotting businessman, I feel as if I'm in a squeeze play most of the time. I'm intent on making it home—sometimes literally my warm and comfortable home where my wife awaits, and always the home that God has prepared for me in heaven—but along the way there's lots to keep me from making it.

At home, I'm surrounded by family and friends of like mind and a shared faith. They understand my desire to obey Christ, to worship Him, to meditate on His word, and to enjoy His blessings. On the road, I'm often going up against tough—almost ruthless—negotiators who couldn't care less about my beliefs. They want to make the deal, and they'll do almost anything to do it.

At home I'm loved, comforted, nurtured, and accepted. On the road I'm buffeted, tempted, rushed, and sometimes rejected.

Most of the time I'm caught between business and home. I'm in a hot box. A rundown. A squeeze play.

Don't get me wrong; I love my work. I've had the privilege of working with some of the most gifted people in television and professional sports in a career that has taken me to dozens of countries on four continents. Along the way I have been fortunate enough to win an Emmy and a few other awards for my work. For the most part it's been rewarding, and even the deals that got away offered an exciting chase. As I stated in my first book, *Roaring Lambs*, I truly believe I was called by God to serve Him in the field of professional sports and television—I'm not trying to get out of my business world.

It's just that as a Christian there is a constant tension between my faith and my work. One minute I'm at a cocktail party in Paris where my host strongly hints that I could have a "companion" waiting for me in my hotel room; the next minute I'm in that hotel room, lonely, missing my wife, wishing I could commiserate with one of my buddies from my Bible study group.

One minute I'm at my desk facing a private meeting where I must fire an employee; the next minute I'm at church trying to sing "It Is Well with My Soul."

One minute I'm in the opulent palace of the Shah of Iran; the next minute I sit down to tuna casserole at my kitchen table.

One minute I'm *Mr.* Briner; the next minute I'm just Dad.

Through my thirty-eight years of charging ahead through these squeeze plays, I've discovered a few ways to help keep things in balance. I've still got a lot to learn, but it occurred to me that there are a lot of Christian men in secular work who might benefit from my many mistakes and occasional triumphs. Perhaps you, too, have felt squeezed to the point where there's no way out. Maybe you feel as if you've failed to keep a heavenly perspective on this difficult game we call life. I'm sure there are those who might even admit to caving in entirely to the pressure your work places on you. I have at times, and it's a lousy feeling.

Relax. No matter where you are in your own "hot box," God can meet you along the base path and lift you up beyond your circumstances. He can carry you safely to your next appointment and protect you with His grace. I know, because I've been there, and just when I took off toward home and saw the sly smile of the catcher holding the perfect throw from the first baseman, God intervened and whispered that word every base runner loves to hear:

"Safe!"

BOB BRINER
DALLAS, TEXAS

# All Alone and Far from Home

*It is not good for the man to be alone.*

GENESIS 2:18

YOU RUSHED TO CATCH a plane this morning, raced through the airport to pick up your rental car, spent the day in a series of meetings, scarfed down a power lunch while negotiating with three clients, went back to an office for more meetings followed by a sumptuous dinner with a prospective client. Then you checked into the hotel, headed up the elevator, walked down the hall and opened the door to your room. After tipping the bellman, the door closed behind you and suddenly, for the first time all day, you were alone.

Really alone.

And after the initial relief, you discovered something. You were lonely.

Next to sexual temptation, loneliness is the weapon of choice used against Christian men in the '90s. The Evil One often combines the despair of loneliness and the false promise of illicit sexual delight into a powerful one-two punch aimed squarely at vulnerable men. Knockouts are scored far too frequently.

As one who has spent thousands of nights in hotel rooms away from my family, I can give firsthand testimony to the difficulty of combating loneliness. It is a real and consistent problem. While I understand the usefulness of Christian retreats, times of solitude, seasons of prayer, contemplation, and study, I can never express the celebration of solitude that I've read about in such books as *Alone at Last*. Greta Garbo's often quoted and misquoted statement, "I want to be left alone," does not resonate with me. I do not want to be alone. I want my wife, my family, my friends.

Despite the sound biblical advice recorded in Genesis that a person ought not be left alone, today's career climate requires that a man be alone a lot. In my business, and I know in many others, travel is one of the prices to be paid for success. You can use the mail, the phone, and the fax only so much. At some point in almost every fruitful business relationship, it is necessary to get on a plane and go meet with your business associate, to see and be seen, face-to-face.

In some countries and cultures, it is mandatory that a personal relationship must be established before any meaningful business is done. And particularly in Asian countries, once that relationship is established, it must be maintained. It cannot be passed off to another colleague, particularly a younger one, lest the original contact be offended. Even within the U.S., most business contacts of any consequence will want to "eyeball" you before a deal is done. And, of course, where detailed and delicate negotiations are involved, sitting down together in the same room, often for marathon sessions, is a must.

Simply put, travel is a fact of business life. And despite great airline schedules, travel often requires overnight stays in hotel rooms. As far as I'm concerned, hotel rooms can be the loneliest places on earth! And the larger the hotel room, the lonelier it feels. I was once given the presidential suite at the Intercontinental Hotel in Budapest. Rattling around alone in that palatial penthouse suite with terraces and balconies overlooking the Danube was one of my life's loneliest interludes.

All the clichés about loneliness are true. It doesn't matter how far away or how near you are to the people who are important to you. Cuba is only ninety miles from the U.S., but I have felt a sharper sense of loneliness and isolation there than in Australia, many thousands of miles and many time zones away. The "lonely in a crowd" cliché is also true. Surrounded by huge crowds in New York, Shanghai, or Moscow, I have felt very alone.

The first step in combating loneliness is to admit you are lonely. This in itself may be tough for many men, because we've been led to believe "real men" don't have such sentimental feelings. Nonsense! You may not cry yourself to sleep at night in the hotel room, but if you're honest with yourself, you'll admit you really miss your family and loved ones. That's okay. In fact, it's perfectly normal. Trying to deny your loneliness only makes you more vulnerable to its harmful effects.

In admitting your loneliness, you'll help prevent the kinds of activities most men take up to cover it up. These include excessive drinking, too much wasted time in front of the television, and dropping your guard when opportunities for inappropriate conduct with other women present themselves to you. When you can't cuddle up to your wife and you're a long way from home, you're pretty vulnerable. The accountability, love, and companionship of family and friends you can count on under normal circumstances is something you don't have when you're on the road.

Some people might tell you that loneliness should not be a problem for Christian men. They might say that you should never feel lonely because God is with you and the Comforter dwells within you. That may be well-intentioned advice, but I've never found it to be of much help. In fact, it could even be a way to rationalize your way around things you shouldn't be doing. That doesn't mean you shouldn't pray, read your Bible, or meditate on the Lord when you sense a bout of loneliness coming on. But if you're like me, you could pray all night and still miss your wife.

That's why I have tried to develop some basic, practical things to do to add substance to my prayers. Maybe they can work for you.

Whenever possible, take a family member along with you on your business trips. I recognize this may not be possible for young men starting out because of the cost. And if you have a young family, having your wife come along with you may seem like an extravagance that is not worth the expense or the trouble in lining up child care. But even if you can only afford to do it once a year, do it!

That one trip together will remain in your memory through all those other lonely trips you take during the year.

As your salary increases and your kids get older, I recommend taking your wife along as often as possible. It's a great way to nurture your relationship and believe me, it's fun! Some of my fondest moments during my marriage have occurred when Marty accompanied me on a business trip.

When your children are old enough, be sure to take each one separately on as many of your business trips as possible. If you travel a lot, you know that those bonus miles add up quickly, allowing your teenager to come along for the price of a few meals. That's a huge bargain when you consider the rewards this produces for you and your children. Not only will you be giving them a tremendous education (travel is a great teacher), but you will solidify your relationship with them. Best of all, you won't be lonely.

Of course, on the vast majority of business travel, you will not have the luxury of taking your wife or children with you. During these times, do the next best thing. Emulate E.T. and phone home. Any company that values its employees will allow them to call home at least once a day at company expense when they are traveling on business. But even if you have to pay for it yourself, make the call; it's worth the three to five dollars. (Remember, your wife is running a corporation, too: your family. She may need to fill you in on some problems she's had. Instead of rattling off your day's accomplishments, be a good listener. Show her you appreciate the great job she's doing. And be honest about your loneliness; tell her you miss her and the kids. The extent to which the two of you connect will determine how effective the call is in fighting off your loneliness.)

Popular radio pastor and author, Chuck Swindoll, has a ritual he follows when traveling which might help you combat loneliness. The first thing he does upon entering his hotel room is to set up a picture of his family on the nightstand near his bed. He says each time he sees it he is reminded of how much he loves his family and of his obligations and promises to them. The photograph probably doesn't make him miss them any less, but it helps fill some of the lonely hours with thoughts of his wife and children.

By all means, use the time alone in your hotel room to get caught up on your Bible reading and prayer, but take some other good reading along too. Through painful experience, I have learned to take about twice as many books as I think I will read on a trip, especially when traveling overseas in non-English-speaking countries where it's difficult to find newspapers and other literature in English. I have spent too many nights in Moscow, Prague, Beijing, and Dubai, kept awake by jet lag and time changes, wracked by boredom, loneliness, and desolation, having exhausted all my reading material. Paperbacks will help lighten the load, but still take more than you think you will need. Then give them away before the return trip.

Another way to combat loneliness is to avoid the temptation to schedule long trips. Long trips may seem to be a more efficient use of your travel budget, but they set you up for the problems associated with loneliness. For me, ten days away from home is the max before I begin to burn out. You may find that it's better to carve a ten-day trip into two five-day trips with a month or so in between.

As a general rule, I recommend to avoid being gone over two weekends. In fact, I try really hard to always be home on weekends, or at least on Sundays, though that's not always possible. Unfortunately, even the airlines are now fighting against businessmen's efforts to join their families for the important weekend days. Tickets are sometimes several hundred dollars cheaper if you stay over Saturday, almost mandating an extra day away for some and making Sunday a day for flying. Both businesses and individuals must count all the costs when calculating the expense of travel. Often the price in terms of well-being for the family is too high to pay for a cheaper airline ticket.

Here are a few other little "tricks" to help you combat loneliness on the road:

- Get enough sleep. Fatigue only compounds loneliness. Turn the television off, read until you're sleepy, call home, then "lights out."
- Stay busy. That's good for business, and it will provide less time for feeling lonely.
- Get some exercise. You've probably spent all day sitting in meetings and eating in fancy restaurants. Take a walk. Do some exercises in your room.
- Write a letter to your family. Go ahead and mail it, even if you'll arrive home before the letter. Even if you don't mail it, the exercise will help.
- Admit your loneliness to a colleague. You're not the only lonely one out there, and talking with a seatmate on your flight about your families will be good

for both of you. Go ahead—take out the pictures and brag a little!

——

Don't take loneliness lightly or be lulled into thinking it is not a weapon which will be used against you and your family. Prepare for an ongoing battle and make sure your wife and children are allies in it. Know your own limits. Don't overextend yourself. Do not cavalierly put yourself in harm's way. Ask for prayer. Pray yourself. In battling loneliness in the right way, you are really defending your home and family as well as your own well-being. The stakes are high. Be ready.

# The Growth Trap

*Watch out! Be on your guard against all kinds of greed; a man's life does not consist in the abundance of his possessions.*

LUKE 12:15

IN A MEMORABLE SCENE from the movie "Arthur," the title character, played by Dudley Moore, asks the bartenders to serve him and his drinking companion another drink. They are obviously already grossly intoxicated, so the bartender asks the classic question all bartenders inevitably ask, "Don't you think you've had enough?"

Arthur's immediate rejoinder is, "I want more than enough."

Do you ever feel that this is what's expected of you? More than enough? "Hey Smith, your sales are down this month." "I'm sorry, Dave, but you haven't logged enough billable hours." "Come on, Jones, we need those reports sooner!"

You're pushing yourself to the limit, yet it isn't enough. More than enough, and then more than that is what the world wants and always will. More!

American business trades on the premise that if you're not growing, you're actually declining. More recently, mere growth isn't even enough. If you grew by five percent last year, you must grow by seven percent this year and ten percent next year.

This is most apparent in the way financial writers analyze companies they cover. A company can go along for years producing a quality product or service, making solid profits and paying its stockholders a solid return on their investments and still be castigated in the financial press. Unless there is growth, earnings are said to be "flat." Unless management is "growing" the company, it is reported to be sleepy, old world, Neanderthal. There is little praise (and almost never a promotion) for the manager that puts quality over profit; who produces a steady, if unspectacular, profit margin for his company's shareholders. It seems as if regular, steady, dependable earnings aren't enough anymore. We need to come up with more.

My associates and I learned the "more" lesson very pointedly through our involvement in building professional tennis. When the leading players of the world initially came to ask for our help they said, "All we want is a regular schedule of tournaments with enough prize money to enable the best players to make a living doing what we do best: playing tennis." Just a place to play and fair pay. That was where we started. When I opted out, players were making millions of dollars in prize money and untold other millions in endorsement income.

Players who once only wanted a place to play were now complaining that rules which required them to play as much as thirteen weeks a year were too onerous. (Who would want to have to travel to places such as Paris, Rome, London, and Monte Carlo to play tennis for as many as thirteen weeks a year to earn only a measly million dollars or so?) I decided it was time to move on when players complained to our board of directors because the free cars they were given to drive at tournaments were only Buicks and not Cadillacs. The players really wanted only one thing: more. I knew that the Cadillac would be followed by a Mercedes, and so on.

It's pretty easy to point fingers at professional athletes and entertainers, but the problem of wanting more than enough plagues all of us, especially anyone who has reached a level of success. You strive for a promotion, get it, are satisfied for a while, but soon you want more. So this time, you want your promotion faster—waiting a year and a half is too long.

Then you start the "I guess I'll reward myself" syndrome by adding to your collection of toys. If the new car doesn't satisfy you, you'll trade it for a sportier model. Or you'll get a boat. But after awhile, twenty-two feet seems too small, so you trade it for a twenty-eight footer. And you know what, you're still not satisfied. So you order a bigger one yet, only this time you need a more powerful motor and a handsomely appointed cabin. But you know what happens next? Even if you own the biggest boat made, it will never be enough.

More than enough is a moving target. We can come close, but we never really hit it. Ross Perot has billions, but it wasn't enough—he also wanted to be president. I've heard people say, "Gee, if I had that kind of money I'd just invest it and go live modestly off the interest." Guess what? No matter how much that annual interest payment would be, you would soon discover it wasn't enough. You'd want just a little more. I think it's pretty telling that so many state lottery winners end up in debt within a few short years after overspending their supposedly limitless supply of cash. More just never seems to be enough.

As a Christian businessman living and working in a society consumed with the "more than enough" attitude, your job will want more than you can give, and you, in turn, will feel as if you deserve more than you can afford. It's the proverbial vicious cycle that forces many men to sacrifice their faith and families on the altar of "more." How tragic to see young men entering the work world and doing what's expected of them, only to discover a few years later that they are trapped with huge mortgages, high monthly payments for expensive toys, sixty-hour weeks, and a growing gap between them and their families. I am honestly convinced that this "more than enough" syndrome is at least partly responsible for so many broken families in the church. Somehow, we've got to resist the pervasive pressure to climb on the bandwagon.

I don't presume to have all the answers on this problem—indeed, I also have to constantly fight the urge to do more and gain more. I have been challenged in my own thinking by Christian writers such as Ron Sider and Gary Moore who offer solid biblical teaching about the dangers of making money into an idol. And, certainly, it is difficult to read the Bible without noticing the many warnings against putting material wealth and blessings at the center of our lives.

American Christians seem to be especially susceptible to the "more than enough" mindset, so, in general, I recommend great caution when it comes to money. It is so easy to believe that God wants us to be the wealthiest people on earth, when all He really wants is our obedience.

Developing the right *attitude* about material wealth takes time, but here are a few things you can do right now that will help you stay out of the "more" trap:

- Face the problem honestly. Admit it—you've got more than you need and you're still thinking about getting more. Most of us like to point to someone who seems to have more money and say, "*They* have a problem." That makes you feel better after you've picked up a new toy, but it doesn't solve *your* problem. Remind yourself daily that you live in a "more than enough" world.

- Count your blessings. I find myself less likely to covet something if I take a look at what I already have. And some of those "things" don't have a price tag: a faithful wife, friends, memories, a personal relationship with God. Who needs the hassle of a new boat if you already don't have enough time to enjoy the things in your life that really count?

- Apply the "zero sum" rule. In terms of material possessions, don't buy anything without getting rid of something. Want a new television? Sell your old one or give it away. New tennis racket? Take the old one (more likely, the four or five old ones) down to the local YMCA. You get the idea.

- Never shop without a specific objective. Window shopping generally results in a purchase. You see something you think you want and out comes the credit card. You're less likely to want more if you stay out of stores.
- Consider renting. A new motor home may cost $50,000 and you'll use it four weeks a year (if you're lucky). You can rent the same motor home for around $500 a week and not have to maintain it, license it, insure it, or store it.
- Invest in time rather than things. Use your expendable income to provide enriching experiences for you and your family. You probably need a weekend retreat with your wife more than you need a new snowmobile. Your children may benefit more from a trip to the ballpark than from yet another video game. Experiences like these result in better relationships and lasting memories.
- Never buy on impulse. If you see something you'd like to buy, go home and sleep on it. Chances are, the urge to have more will pass. Notice how the things you really *need* you think about and research before you make the purchase, while the things you *want* are bought on the spot.
- Form an accountability relationship with someone who will give you honest feedback on your handling of material blessings. I know of an individual who regularly opens his checkbook to a friend as a way of holding himself accountable for the way he spends his money. Ouch! That's allowing yourself to be

pretty vulnerable, and I'm not sure I even recommend it. I mention it only to show how seriously some people take this problem, and to urge you to do something extraordinary to make sure your priorities are in the right place.

Please understand that I'm not advocating a "no growth" position or asking you to live like a hermit. I shudder to think what the Christian community would look like if we all eschewed the earning of money. And as a businessman, I know the importance of growth, and I do my best to help my company earn more this year than they did last year. Excellence should always be our goal as Christian businessmen, for our work is one way in which we can honor Christ.

The ability to earn money and use it properly is what stewardship is all about. I fully subscribe to John Wesley's admonition to earn all you can and save all you can so that you may give all you can. We must, however, understand that the only "more" which will really satisfy us is more of God in our lives. He, and He alone, can quench our thirst for more.

Don't feel guilty about what you already have. Even if you've been trapped by the attitude of "more is not enough," now you can be free of the pressure to work more so that you can buy more. You can take control over your resources and simplify your life. You can experience the pleasure that comes from spending time instead of spending money. And you can enjoy the genuine satisfaction that comes from seeking more of God.

Begin today. Set aside a few minutes to reflect on all that you have. Be thankful for the simple things that have been buried by all that you have accumulated. Then call your wife and make a date for the two of you to take a walk in the park. They could be your first steps toward a care-free and uncluttered life!

# Don't Take It Personally

——

*Better a little with righteousness than much gain with injustice.*

A LONGTIME FRIEND, one who my partner and I had helped along the way in his career, told us he decided to award valuable television rights he controlled to our major competitor—instead of to our company. No explanation. No chance to compete with the other company. Just an abrupt "hasta la vista." Another friend, whose career as a sportscaster we helped build by continually putting him on the air when no one else knew him, selected another company to manage his career after he had achieved a measure of stardom. Again, it was abruptly done with no opportunity to make a counter offer.

Both men rationalized their decisions by telling us it was a business decision. "Don't take it personally," they both said, probably noticing that we were indeed taking it personally. Although we have had many business dealings with this sportscaster since that incident and have an easy, ongoing relationship with him, the bond of trust between us is no longer nearly as strong. And the same could be said of our other former client.

Some things you can't help but take personally.

—　—

One of the most repeated admonitions you hear in the business world is this: keep your business and personal lives separate. I don't believe it's good advice or even possible, but it's advice you've probably heard and are trying to follow. You'd be better off trying to build a tower out of sand, because the more you try to "not get personal" in your business dealings, the more schizophrenic you'll become.

Call me old-fashioned, but I believe that nearly all our dealings in business are built on relationships. When I go after a prospective client, I do everything I can to establish a relationship. This isn't a ploy to get his business. It's a natural extension of who we are as humans—social animals who delight in building friendships with others. I enjoy meeting new people and learning more about them, and I trust they have enjoyed getting to know me as well. It's what makes business so rewarding. In fact, if you don't really enjoy developing relationships with people, you probably are in the wrong line of work. Business *is* relationships.

I believe a good deal of this "don't take it personally" approach is motivated by a very cynical and selfish view of business that stems from unscrupulous exploitation of customers who are seen only as a source of profit. Sure, you court your client, make him think you're his friend, even send him a birthday card or inquire about his family. But he's important only as long as he buys your product or hires your company for its services. If something comes up that terminates the relationship, "Hey! Don't take it personally."

I recall hearing a story about a salesman who, when he called on his accounts, always inquired about his clients' children. Most customers responded politely with a "they're just fine, thank you," but one customer always went on for about twenty minutes, updating the salesman about his son and daughters. The salesman's supervisor rode along with him once, and after visiting the "talkative" client he warned the salesman to avoid taking so much company time for chit-chat. "Oh, but I couldn't do that," responded the salesman. "You'd lose a customer and I'd lose a friend."

I like that, and I believe there's a place for such an attitude in business. As Christians, we ought to lead the way in making business more personable. In the short run, it will make you more successful, because once you view clients as friends, you will do everything you can to help them succeed. They, in turn, will reward you with their loyalty—and when they don't, it's *okay* to take it personally.

Mixing business interests with your personal life will benefit you in more than just the short-term. In the long run, it will pay off in kingdom benefits. Showing a customer kindness and respect, being willing to get involved with him or her on a personal basis, will make him or her more likely to approach you in times of personal crises. Then you will be right where God has called you, positioned to extend His grace and peace.

I can almost hear you objecting: "Briner, are you ever naive! You've got to be the biggest sucker around." I don't blame you for thinking that because we've all been conditioned to think being nice means being soft. Hardly. I've had to go toe-to-toe in knock-down negotiations with people whom I consider to be friends. Most of the time I win, but sometimes I lose. But either way, "taking it personally" can be a benefit. Some of my fondest moments in the business have come after tough negotiations when the guy on the other side of the table says, "Well, RAB, you won this time, so I guess you won't mind buying me lunch tomorrow." And we leave the table as we approached it: as friends who respect each other and don't allow the necessities of business to interfere with that friendship.

Does "making it personal" have its downside? Certainly. The stories I recounted at the beginning of this chapter bear witness to the fact if you form personal relationships with your business associates sometimes your feelings may get hurt. It's hard to have the same level of friendship with a colleague after he takes his business elsewhere or even disagrees with you in a meeting. The alternative, however, is too unattractive. I would rather risk a few of those touchy situations than to begin treating every client and colleague as an object.

As far as I'm concerned, it's about as difficult to separate your business and personal interests as it is to separate your faith from the real world. It's next to impossible to be a businessman one moment and a person with emotions and feelings the next. Those who try not to take it personally eventually become dishonest. They burn out faster, turn to alcohol and other distractions more frequently, and tend to change jobs more often. I'd much rather enjoy my work, and "taking it personally" helps.

—▪—

Your career is tough enough without attempting to go it alone. Buck conventional wisdom and begin looking at your colleagues and clients as real people. Be a risk-taker and allow yourself to get involved in their world. Get to know them as fathers, husbands, softball players, coin collectors, etc., instead of seeing them as only account numbers. Your work will be more rewarding, and, mark my words, someday one of these "clients" will ask you what it is that makes you seem so personable.

# Back to the Basics

—▬—

*Do everything without complaining or arguing, so
that you may become blameless and pure, children of
God without fault in a crooked and depraved gen-
eration, in which you shine like stars in the universe
as you hold out the word of life. . . .*

PHILIPPIANS 2:14–16A

RECENTLY, I WAS ON a cross-country flight and happened to
be seated next to Gordon Jump, the television personality
("WKRP In Cincinnati" and  ubiquitous "Maytag repair-
man" of the Maytag commercials). Because we were in the
first-class cabin, we received a great deal of attention and
service from the flight attendants. I did not feel I was being
overly polite, but Jump, who previously hadn't said a word,
remarked to me, "I can't help but notice how kind you are
to the flight attendant. You have thanked her every time
she has done the least little thing for you. She is only doing
her job, but you seem so appreciative. Why?"

Even though I was totally unprepared for his question,
it gave me a great opportunity to share my faith and answer
many subsequent questions he had about a commitment to
Christ.

—▬—

The general decline in basic civility and personal integrity, as lamentable as it is, presents a wonderful oppor-

tunity for modern Christians—particularly for Christian businessmen. Christians can have a very positive impact by learning to exercise what were once just ordinary standards of courtesy toward those with whom we do business. We can literally "shine like stars," to use the beautiful phrase from Philippians, as our behavior contrasts so vividly with that of other people in business. In a business climate that is coarse, rude, and basically unresponsive, we can stand out by becoming people of very good, even excellent, manners and by performing up to a higher standard of professional behavior.

My business and nonbusiness activities bring me into contact with a wide variety of people, from the most secular in my television business activities, to many Christians as I serve on church-related boards and commissions and write for Christian publications. I am sorry to say that there is very little difference between the business manners of Christians and non-Christians. In fact, I must sadly admit that, overall, non-Christians perform better. Yet, if any group should be concerned about relating positively and politely to those around them, sending signals of caring commitment to quality relationships, it should be Christians in business. There is a tremendous need for Christians to stand out and make a difference.

The reason to learn and exercise impeccable business manners and to be more aware of our responsibilities and opportunities in this area is not to attain a superficial patina of sophistication or gentility. It is not even to enhance our business standing, although that is an inevitable result. It is, rather, to very consciously become better, more visible, more effective representatives of the Savior as we demonstrate care toward people (which is the essence of good manners) both in the business sphere and in all other areas of our lives.

Here are three seemingly basic things that will help you "shine like stars" and become better representatives of the Savior.

First, do what you say you will do. The ninth commandment tells us not to lie. You may think you are a very truthful person, but every time you do not do what you say you will do, you tell a lie. Particularly in business, we have become cavalier about doing what we say we will do. "I'll call you tomorrow." "We'll get together soon for lunch." "I will shoot you a fax on that ASAP." "I will be there at 10 A.M. sharp." "You'll have a signed contract on your desk by noon Monday." Too often, we make these kinds of statements without a real commitment to being sure we do our part in making them happen.

Unfortunately, Christians in business can be as bad about not making promised calls, not delivering as promised, not being punctual—not doing what we say we will do—as non-Christians. While there will be some circumstances beyond our control that prevent us from doing what we say we will do, these should be rare exceptions, not the rule. And when they do occur, we should be very quick to apologize and make it very clear that we are disappointed that our performance has not measured up to our promise.

Many Christians, with the best of intentions and motives, may also overcommit and overpromise. But good intentions really do not absolve us. I have one dear Christian friend and business associate who repeatedly tells me, "I really meant to call you yesterday, but. . . ." Always a "but." The best of motives does not make up for lack of follow-through. Our call is to a higher standard.

The second basic area of conduct I ask you to consider is that of always speaking when spoken to. I am sure you will be initially puzzled by my concerns here. Most everyone will say, "Of course, I speak when I am spoken to. To ignore someone speaking to me would be unbelievably rude. I would never do that." Yet, failing to return phone calls, answer messages, or reply to letters is actually more rude than ignoring someone speaking directly to us.

Think of the effort and expense involved in making a phone call, sending a fax, writing a letter, or leaving a message. A person who has done any one of these has gone to much greater lengths to communicate than someone who speaks directly to you. Why, then, do we so often fail to respond, particularly in a timely way, to these kinds of communications?

I have had people tell me, "I just don't write letters," or "I am not a very good correspondent." They seem to think this absolves them from failing to communicate, failing to speak when spoken to. It doesn't. From personal experience, I know that very positive changes can be made in one's letter-answering habits. For many years, I was a terrible correspondent. To this day, I am still ashamed that I did such a poor job writing to my parents during my college years. They sacrificed in order to help me attend a Christian college, yet I couldn't be bothered to write them once a week. Terrible. Even in my first career years I was a lousy correspondent, both on a personal and a business basis.

That all changed, however, when I moved to New Orleans to work for the governor of Louisiana in developing and building the Superdome. In the very early days of that job, God told me that if I was going to do the job right, I would have to become a much better correspondent. I still remember the day in 1967 that I resolved to make every effort to answer each letter the same day I received it. That resolve still holds, to the point that it makes me very uncomfortable to have unanswered letters on my desk.

Am I one hundred percent successful in always answering a letter the day I receive it? Of course not. Travel and other commitments interfere, and I do not always get it done. It is surprising, however, how often my commitment helps me to get it done on a daily basis and how it always helps me to get it done sooner than my old laissez-faire attitude would.

Taking care of correspondence in a timely way is wonderfully liberating. To not have a stack of unanswered letters on your desk reminding you of your negligence allows you to get on with the rest of your work in a more relaxed, productive way. Also, answering mail as it is received is the most efficient way to deal with it. The letter is there, you answer it, it is done, and you move on. And anyone can institute this system; it's simply a matter of commitment.

The third area of conduct to which I would like to draw your attention is the area of saying thanks. Christians, of all people, should be the most expert at saying thanks. After all, we have the most for which to be thankful. We need to be in a constant attitude of thanksgiving toward God the Father for all His blessings to us, and particularly for the gift of His Son.

This attitude of thanksgiving and the habit of expressing thanks should carry over into all areas of our lives, and has particular importance to business. As a Christian in business, you should look for every opportunity to say thanks to those with whom you come in contact. Also be alert for chances to express your gratitude to those who have helped or extended a courtesy or a kindness.

Among the people I try hard to remember to thank are the secretaries of my business associates who do so much to help facilitate things and ease the problems of doing business. A word of thanks, a note, a card, is very much appreciated and will set you apart as someone who cares about them.

An important aspect of saying thanks effectively is timeliness. In my business, we often send gifts ordered from catalogs. It is amazing to me that even with rather expensive gifts, gifts that had to be pretty much unexpected, to Christians and non-Christians alike, it is often necessary to go back to the catalog company to verify delivery because no word of thanks from the recipient has been forthcoming. To receive a gift, a business favor, or any other personal kindness and not offer thanks as quickly as possible significantly devalues your expression of gratitude. After leaving a particularly good business meeting or one in which a kindness has been extended to me, I will often go to a phone and dictate a message of thanks to be faxed immediately to the appropriate people. To paraphrase the quotation which says, "Justice delayed is justice denied" we should remember that "thanks delayed is thanks diminished." Be prompt. Say thanks.

—  —

When you do what you say you will do, when you speak when spoken to, and when you say thanks, you express a concern for others that is consistent with being a Christian. This is the way you can shine like a star. Begin today to correct old habits of neglecting these three important areas. In doing so, you will represent the excellence of the Savior.

# One of the Boys

—-—

*You are the salt of the earth. But if the salt lose its saltiness, how can it be made salty again? . . . let your light shine before men.*

SOONER OR LATER, in almost any field, you'll be faced with some basic lifestyle choices. You'll come to a time when you must decide if your behavior will be significantly different from the behavior of those who do not profess Christ. Usually these decisions are brought about by incidents involving alcohol, foul language and stories, and the kind of generally lewd behavior one might expect in a high school locker room. On the surface this rather common behavior among men—especially men away from home— seems pretty harmless, and I almost hesitate to even bring it up. After all, we're grown-ups here, right? Boys will be boys? We deserve a little fun and games?

I'm not here to tell you how to live your life, and I don't intend to pull a legalistic maneuver on you. I'm well aware of how some people make these issues a matter of whether you're a Christian or not, a position that I don't necessarily share. But I do believe that part of the struggle between faith and career includes a strong pull to buy into the lifestyle of those with whom we work. Sell out here and it's easier to compromise on other, more important issues.

— —

I was only a few months off the campus of Spring Arbor College, a small conservative Christian college in Michigan, when I arrived in Miami to join the franchise that would become the Miami Dolphins. As one Michigan newspaper wrote about the move, "It is about 2,000 miles from Michigan to south Florida, but it is light years from Spring Arbor College to professional football in Miami." How true.

My title with the Dolphins was promotional director, but my real job was to build solid, positive relationships between the team and the Miami press corps. If the new franchise was to succeed, good press relations, particularly with the powerful *Miami Herald*, were a must. The two key writers, the lead "beat" man and the star columnist, were both hard-drinking, high-living bachelors. They became *my* primary beat!

Their frequent nights out were musts for me. At first I thought it was amazing how popular I was. They always wanted me to tag along. Then it dawned on me that the writers realized a night of sipping Cokes did not impair my driving ability. I was their designated driver before the term was even coined. So much for my popularity.

Those nights out with my press friends were exciting and glamorous. Legendary writers and broadcasters from the north, down to cover the racing season or baseball's spring training, would often join our group. Red Smith,

Curt Gowdy, Red Barber, and other sports media giants were often with us for the evening. Pretty heady stuff for a kid from a small Christian college.

But they were also very troubling times; scary times, spiritually speaking. I had gone to Miami to try my best at succeeding in professional sports. I had also determined to continue to try and live out the Christian life, to represent the Savior. But to be a success, I was now hanging out at places like the El Bolero, Julie's Pad, the Bonfire, and other legendary Miami watering holes. The alcohol flowed, the conversation was witty yet often vulgar, and women were always around and available.

Luckily, alcohol wasn't a problem. I did not drink before or during my days in Miami and have not done so since. Staying away from alcohol has never, I repeat, *never*, negatively affected my career. In fact, not drinking has been a plus. The women were a temptation, but God helped me handle it. And I tried to distance myself from the vulgar language and crude jokes.

Still, I had tremendous doubts and fears. Was this the right kind of environment for a Christian? Could I be deeply involved in the world and yet not really be a part of it? Did my being there really help advance the cause of Christ?

I guess each man has to answer those questions for himself, but for me, the answer has played itself out in the years since those early days in Miami. One of those two key writers is now one of America's most honored sportswriters. But he's also an active member of one of south Florida's most dynamic churches, has a portion of a library named for him at a Christian college, his son is a classmate of my daughter's at that same college, and he and his wife have blessed our family with a rich, rewarding, ongoing Christian fellowship.

Do I take credit for this? No, the credit goes entirely to God, who guided my steps to Miami and protected me from temptation. I have since come to believe that Christians indeed need to be willing to enter places where sin abounds. As I wrote in *Roaring Lambs*, we expect our culture to share our values, but we have fled too often from those culture-shaping arenas and retreated into our Christian ghettoes. True, I could have been won over by the glitz and glamour of the Miami night life, but sooner or later, God would have found someone to live out the gospel so that an influential sportswriter would find Christ.

If you are in a situation where there is constant pressure to become one of the boys, I hope my story will inspire you to hold dearly to your principles. The very people trying to get you to take your first drink want desperately to find someone who is for real. You may endure some kidding, but you will be respected if you refuse to let a waitress sit on your lap or you walk away when the stories go foul. In the end, you will feel better about yourself and may even, as I did, see one of your colleagues come to faith.

—  —

I've been "one of the boys" throughout most of my professional career, yet I've never had to drink, gamble, or carouse with them. You don't have to do those things to get ahead. You can stay away from destructive habits and still have fun and be included in circles of influence. It's a myth of the Enemy that tells you otherwise. Stay clean. Stay sober. Be a beacon to those around you who are in the dark.

# Worshiping at Bedside Baptist

—▪—

*There remains then, a sabbath-rest for the people of God; for anyone who enters God's rest also rests from his own work, just as God did from his.*

HEBREWS 4:9–10

MY PLANE LANDED at Hong Kong's International Airport and a limo was waiting for me when I cleared customs. We zipped across town to my hotel where I barely had enough time to check in and freshen up before it was time to climb back into the limo and head over to the headquarters of a major advertiser to discuss promotion of a potential new basketball league. Over lunch we were joined by some community leaders who wanted to know more about establishing a franchise in Hong Kong, then it was out the door for a series of meetings with television people. By the time I fell into my bed later that evening, it dawned on me. I had just worked through another Sunday and never had the opportunity to worship.

—▪—

One of the hazards of today's fast-paced business world is the seven-day work week. Especially on the international scene, Sunday is just another day in which to close a deal, check on production values at the plant, or travel to the next appointment. I believe this can be hard on anyone, but it is especially difficult on Christians because we know how much we need to be connected with other believers through worship experiences.

Although I believe it is possible to worship "on the run," regular church attendance is far better. I need the ritual of seeing friends as I enter my little church, taking my place in the pew, singing the great hymns of the church, participating in the reading of Scripture, and being challenged and instructed by a message from God's word delivered by my pastor. To me, it is no accident that we Christians refer to our churches as "sanctuaries," for it is within their comforting walls that I am protected from all the stress and excitement of my work.

I wish it were possible for me to be in church every Sunday, but it isn't. Try as I might to schedule meetings during the weekday, more often than not I have to be out of town, far from my home church on Sunday mornings. That is probably true for you, too. To be successful in most lines of work means you have to travel, and you can't always get back home on weekends. Naturally, this can take its toll on family relationships, but it can also torpedo your spiritual life. It's hard enough fighting the temptations that come with the turf, let alone trying to maintain a vibrant worship life. But there *are* some things you can do to minimize the effect of being absent from your church on Sunday morning.

First, try to attend *some* church. That's a tough one, I'll admit. I've arrived at my hotel room late on a Saturday night when my body is still in another time zone, and when I wake up the next morning it takes a lot of discipline to roll out and head for a church I know nothing about. On the other hand, the times I've done that have been extremely rewarding.

Most hotels in the United States offer church directories that will at least serve as a partial "menu." Generally these churches represent the "mainline" or more liberal traditions, but I've found that these churches minister to me if only by providing a quiet setting where I can meditate, read from my Bible, and praise God by singing hymns. Then, too, the experience of worshiping in a different environment and observing others' traditions can add a new dimension to your faith.

Overseas, you will often find English-speaking churches that minister to "ex-pats" who live and work there. These congregations are usually nondenominational in nature and can be wonderfully enriching. I've found that Anglican churches overseas tend to be more evangelical than one might expect, and that their congregations are often a wide mix of people from varied church backgrounds. It's interesting to see how denominational differences seem to melt away in places where Christianity is the minority religion.

Still, there will be times when you absolutely cannot make it to church. In some Muslim countries, Christian churches are either illegal or so highly monitored that it is wise to keep your distance. Or you may simply be too tired or be traveling. The important thing is to find ways to fill the void left from not attending church. Here are just a few things that may help:

- *Join the electronic church.* Televangelists and their electronic ministries are an easy target, but don't let the failures of a few flamboyant and unscrupulous TV preachers turn you off to radio or television ministries. As far as I'm concerned, the greatest value of electronic ministries is that they reach people who cannot or will not attend church. In virtually any city in the United States you can find a radio broadcast of a local, Bible-believing church's Sunday-morning worship service. Many times you can also find a local church's worship service on television. If it's impossible for you to attend church on a business trip, at least flip on the TV or radio and join in worship.

- *Carry taped sermons with you.* Check with your own home church to see if they tape Sunday services for shut-ins. If they do, pick a few up and put them in your briefcase before a business trip. Even if it's a sermon you've heard before, it's nice to hear a familiar voice and to sing along with your congregation. For a small donation, most radio and television ministries will send you a tape of their broadcasts, also an excellent alternative to attending church on the road.

- *Worship with music.* Music is so much a part of worship. David exhorts us to "Sing joyfully to the LORD" (Psalm 33:1). Take along tapes of praise music and listen to them when you can't attend church. At 35,000 feet, you can be in your own magnificent sanctuary with a Walkman, listening to great anthems of praise and worship to the Almighty.

- *Conduct your own church service.* This is especially helpful if you are traveling with other believers. Gather with them for a time of praying, sharing, and reading the Bible together. If you are alone, spend some extra time in your personal devotions when you can't attend church.

- *Let your environment minister to you.* If you're flying over the mountains or the ocean on a Sunday morning, focus on God's creative power and remind yourself that even now He is watching over you. If you're stuck in traffic in a foreign capital, try to view the crush of humanity as Jesus would. Use the time to pray and meditate on God's desire that all people should be saved. If you find yourself in the sterile environment of an airport or hotel lobby, remind yourself that Jesus was forced to spend time in the wilderness. Allow your surroundings on Sunday to focus your attention on the Master.

- *Ask others to pray for you.* Whenever you know you will have to miss church due to business, call your pastor and ask him to pray for you. Confess your need to your Sunday school class or Bible-study group. It has been a great comfort to me to know that even as I am absent from the caring environment of my local church, my Christian brothers and sisters are praying for me.

None of these options is an adequate substitute for actually being in church, but they help. If you're not careful, a Sunday on a business trip can become just another work day, or simply a good day to sleep in and then take in some of the local sights. By all means, your Sunday on the road—just as at home—should be a day of rest and rejuvenation. But I believe it also should be a day when you spend more time than usual worshiping God and learning about Him from His Word. If you don't take it upon yourself to do something special on the Sundays you're on the road, you deprive yourself of the blessings God intends you to have.

— —

If your work forces you to miss church, take comfort in knowing you're not alone. Thousands of believers struggle with this, and more will join them as our society increasingly views Sunday as another workday. I've had the pleasure of observing various "sports chapels" conducted before professional athletic contests, and I know how important they are to Christian ballplayers who have to take the field on the Lord's day. You will reap the same benefits if you incorporate some creative worship experiences into the next business trip that keeps you away from church on Sunday. You deserve the spiritual boost that comes with worshiping, so on your next business trip over a weekend, don't just sleep in. Worship the King!

# Is It Right to Fire an Employee?

—▬—

*Masters, provide your slaves with what is right and fair, because you know that you also have a Master in heaven.*

Colossians 4:1

I KNEW I NEEDED to fire an executive secretary as soon as I returned from an overseas trip. She had not been honest in performing her duties and had been the source of conflict in the office. For many managers, this would have been an easy decision. She was negligent, had been warned, and now it was time to act. But for me it wasn't easy. I'm not sure firing an employee is ever a cut-and-dried decision, but this situation gave me great heartache. Have you ever wished you never had to make a decision that would terminate an employee?

To fire her and replace her with a more truthful employee able to get along better with her coworkers was the obvious move from a business standpoint. After all, it wouldn't be fair to our other employees to let her "get away with" unprofessional behavior, which made their lives difficult, and with dishonesty, which reflected badly on our company overall. Legally, I was protected. I had done my homework by documenting her problems and giving her repeated written notifications of what she needed to do in order to keep her job. This really was a no-brainer, the type of decision I ought to have been able to make in my sleep.

On the other hand, I really do care about all of my employees, something that I think ought to be the hallmark of every Christian manager. Firing her would create a financial burden for her family. It would be a blow to her self-esteem and a black mark on her work record. More troubling for me, however, was the fact that she was not a Christian and had just begun to talk about spiritual matters with the office staff. (The majority of the people in my office are Christians.) Firing her would remove her from any Christian influence in her life, and I wasn't eager to be the one to do that.

Here was one of those cases where an obvious business decision becomes more complex for a manager who is a Christian. I was caught between my faith and the workplace.

In business, good management begins with good people. If you hire and hold on to good people, your chances of success go up tremendously. Conversely, incompetent employees will stand in the way of your advancement and success. Unfortunately, building an organization of good people requires both hiring and firing.

A Christian manager has all the responsibilities any manager must face, all the different publics he must serve, and the even greater responsibility of integrating his policies, particularly those which directly impact people's lives, with his overriding responsibility to help build God's kingdom.

I recall a friend talking about a manager in the McDonald's chain who was having a problem with a couple of his employees. McDonald's has some pretty high standards for their employees, and these kids fell about a mile short. They came to work late, they were slow (something the fast-food business doesn't tolerate), and they just didn't seem to care about their jobs. When my friend asked the manager why he didn't just fire them (McDonald's is usually pretty swift in booting lousy workers), the manager replied, "I think I'm the only Christian they know. I'm going to work with them as long as I can because I have a lot of positive influence on them." When my friend pressed him, asking if he wasn't worried about his own reputation as a manager, he replied, "Some things are more important than a job."

Now, I realize we have to be good stewards of the trust our companies place in us, and that we should not try to turn a profitable business into a missionary organization, but I must admit I admire that manager, even though I don't agree completely with his reasoning. Every business has a moral obligation to seek the best for its employees; therefore, firing should always be a last resort. The extra effort invested in a substandard employee will eventually benefit the company and community. From a Christian perspective, it may also point that employee toward the Savior.

The Bible does not say much about hiring and firing employees, but it does say plenty about fairness. As Christians, we are expected to go the extra mile with employees whose performances are not acceptable. An employee, after all, is a person, not a number; a soul rather than a "labor unit." At the same time, however, fairness also means giving truthful evaluations, early warnings, mapping out ways to improve, and then, if the employee does not respond, terminating the relationship with as much grace as possible. In that case, we are being fair to other employees who *are* performing well and to those who have a financial interest in the company. And in terms of our faith, we are communicating the important truth that people of God are people committed to excellence.

Fortunately, more and more resources have become available to those who have to make personnel decisions. If your company has a human resources department, make sure you consult with them. They will coach you along the way and help you see the situation objectively. They will also emphasize the importance of documenting problems and giving consistent evaluations aimed at helping the employee succeed. In this day of acute shortages of qualified people, the current trend is to "redeem" employees by finding ways to help them overcome their deficiencies.

My hunch is that the biggest reason most managers waffle when it comes to personnel issues is that they have been lax in handling problems when they first appear. My friends in the labor relations community tell me that most managers do not follow through on giving employees early and honest feedback about their performance. Instead, they tend to let things go until the situation becomes intolerable, and then either fire abruptly or keep the employee with all his or her faults. Neither option serves anyone and only leads to increased stress for the manager. Even a bad decision is better than indecision.

Here, again, is where I believe Christian managers cannot afford to be unprofessional. Even put in the unpleasant situation of confronting an employee about substandard performance, you can shine. Set the example and show others that you care enough about people to handle their employment with "tough love." Whether or not you have to actually let an employee go, the way you approach the problem will say a lot about your faith.

Here are just a few of the issues you might face in the firing of an employee:

- Am I placing too high a priority on business matters over spiritual issues?
- Have I honestly tried to go the extra mile?
- Would it be more redemptive to keep the employee but place him in a position of lesser responsibility?
- If the performance of a Christian employee were the same, would I fire *her*?
- Is it Christian to follow the contemporary advice to fire an employee abruptly and with little explanation other than official performance review results?
- How do I put the truth on an employee's personnel file without jeopardizing his or her chances for future employment?

In the end, I did end up firing the executive secretary. And even though it is always difficult to sit across the desk from someone you are letting go, knowing that I honestly tried to help her keep her job made it a little easier. Hopefully, she was able to see my faith through my honest evaluations, my recommendations for improvement, and what I hope was a compassionate, sensitive meeting where she learned my decision.

Did I do the right thing? I don't pretend to be smart enough to know. I take comfort in knowing that indecision usually makes matters worse and that even struggling with the issue is better than whimsically firing someone who messes up or letting him or her continue to cause problems for your company.

In the end, as we always need to do, I had to rely not on my own experience as a manager, but on the Holy Spirit. If we do our best to present the Savior and His message of salvation, try to live as consistently as our human frailties allow, and bathe our decisions in prayer, we have done the best we can do. The results need to be left with Him.

—•—

Being a Christian in the rough and tumble of the business and professional world is not easy, but peace is available through the knowledge that God does not require us to be brilliant or effective. He asks us only to be obedient and trusting. You can, with His help, turn something as unpleasant as firing an employee into a signpost that points toward the Savior. Your spirit and motives will always be evident. Bring them in line with the God who gives second chances, and even this aspect of your work will glorify Him.

# Those Weird Friends of Yours

*Therefore, as God's chosen people, holy and dearly loved, clothe yourselves with compassion, kindness, humility, gentleness and patience. Bear with each other and forgive whatever grievances you may have against one another.*

COLOSSIANS 3:12–13

IN THE 1970S, WHEN we were building the worldwide professional tennis circuit, I did a tremendous amount of traveling. At one time we had more than ninety professional events making up the Grand Prix circuit being held in cities on every continent.

During one of those years, I decided to keep a log, a record that would show where I had spent each day of that particular year. I found I had spent the most time in my home city of Dallas, but not by much. London was second, with New York and Paris third and fourth.

Near the end of that year, while flying from London to Dallas, I was going over my log making additional entries. My seatmate, a gentleman I did not know, asked what I was doing. When I told him, he asked to see the log. He saw all the capitals of the world—London, Paris, Rome, Moscow, Tokyo, Buenos Aires, Stockholm, Tel-Aviv—and the exotic places—Dubai, Bangalore, Beijing, Shanghai, Hong Kong, Kuala Lumpur—as well as the more prosaic cities listed. After awhile, he looked at me and said, "I would like to visit every city on your list except for McPherson, Kansas, and Greenville, Illinois." When I told him those were my two favorite places to visit, he wanted to know why.

Now, I would be the first to admit that next to Paris and Tokyo, McPherson, Kansas, and Greenville, Illinois, seem out of place. But I dove in and gave him probably more of an explanation than he had wanted. I told him that I had attended Christian colleges in both places and that each held special memories for me. He said, "What is a Christian college? Is it where you study for the priesthood?" I am not sure that my explanation was too cogent. I told him that a Christian college is a school where Christ and His teachings are central to all that goes on and that, yes, it is a place where you study for the priesthood, in the sense that every believer has priestly rights and responsibilities.

He said he could understand nostalgic feelings for one's college days, but couldn't understand why I would continue to return several times a year during all these years, especially when I was doing so much other more attractive traveling. I told him that I needed the contact and fellowship with the people in McPherson and Greenville, to be with like-minded people who shared a faith in Christ. He quickly put his earphones on and began to watch the in-flight movie.

— —

The world does not understand Christian fellowship, but we need to be sure we do. We need to place a high value on it and make sure we both give and receive it.

Without regular, meaningful relationships with other Christians built on accountability and caring, we can never live the joyful kingdom-building life God intends for us to live.

This is especially important for the Christian who spends a good deal of time on the road. Many of your associates will be people who either do not understand your Christian faith or who are openly antagonistic toward it. And much of your time will be spent on topics and situations that are far removed from the classic themes of our faith: love, forgiveness, compassion, peace, contentment, obedience, etc. If you do not "program" Christian fellowship into your life, you will soon begin to think and act like those colleagues who are not followers of Jesus. I have seen it happen, and I know that if I am not careful, it will happen with me.

In the early days of my career, I was something of a black sheep as far as the church was concerned. As much as I love the Christian colleges I attended, it was clear that those who chose the professional ministry as a career track were highest on the pecking order. They were the real Christians. Other acceptable careers included the helping professions such as teaching or social work. But if you even dared express an interest in professional sports or entertainment, you might as well have worn a sign that read "pagan"!

So you can imagine what my church and college friends must have thought when they heard "Briner's working for the Miami Dolphins." The first strike against me was that this was big-time sports. People bet on football games.

They sold beer in the stadium. Most of the people associated with professional sports were womanizers and carousers. And worst of all, the games were played on Sunday!

To tell you the truth, I would never have made it spiritually were it not for a couple of men who refused to believe such nonsense about professional sports and decided to take me under their wing. They prayed with me, called me with words of encouragement, and tried to meet with me whenever possible. For awhile, they *were* my church, my only source of Christian fellowship outside my immediate family of a dedicated wife and three small children.

Times have changed and the church has matured. For better or for worse, a lot of us work in professions that are not traditionally thought of as "ministry," yet the church has done a good job of acknowledging that we are all ministers. But the need for Christian fellowship among those who spend most of their time in a secular setting is still critical. While each person must develop and participate in his own special network of believers, here are some things that have worked for me:

- Join a church. Don't just attend when you can, but take the steps required to become a full member. Membership indeed has its privileges. Even if you cannot attend regularly, it's good to be connected. When you're home for Christmas, you'll love attending the many special services and fellowship opportunities at church during that season. And you'll appreciate knowing a body of believers is praying for you while you travel.

- Get close to your pastor. Take him to lunch and explain that your work will keep you away much of the time but that you desire to be a part of the church. Agree to meet often for prayer and encouragement.
- Develop a few key relationships with trusted Christian friends. Meet as often as possible with one or two friends with whom you can pray, read Scripture, and discuss your faith.
- Visit a church while traveling. Those serendipitous times of worship and meeting new Christian friends will help keep you centered.
- Combine fellowship with fun. Christian fellowship is more than prayer and Bible study. Have fun with your Christian friends. I love taking a fishing trip with a close Christian brother or having some friends from church over for an evening of silliness. Don't mislead yourself or others into thinking Christians never have any fun.

It is no secret that men have a difficult time forming close, personal relationships, and Christian men are no different. As the churches in our neighborhoods become bigger and more professional, it is becoming easier to be an anonymous believer who slips into his seat on Sunday and then leaves without speaking to anyone (or being spoken to). Yet we are missing out on a great blessing when we go it alone or merely maintain superficial relationships with other believers.

I sometimes wonder where I might be today were it not for those few friends who embraced me. And I wonder about other men who do not have the benefit of good, positive, Christian fellowship. As you contemplate your own level of fellowship, ask yourself the following questions:

1.  Do I have a close friend who is a Christian?
2.  Could I share my most private thoughts and feelings with this person?
3.  Do I meet regularly with another Christian to pray and reflect on what God is doing in our lives?
4.  Do I do anything with another Christian that is strictly for fun (such as fishing or going to a ballgame)?
5.  Has another Christian come to me with a serious problem and asked me to help him with it?

If you answered "no" to a majority of these questions, you are missing out on a great resource that will make the struggle between work and home more manageable.

Every chance I get, I make the trip back to McPherson and Greenville. Neither place is easy to get to, but it's worth the extra effort. When I show up at Sony's offices in Japan, I'm Mr. Briner and I have to be "on" all the time. But when I walk across the campus of Greenville College or step into the gym at Central College, I'm not only plain old Bob, I'm the kid they prayed for and still pray for. And I'm among the best friends anyone could hope to have.

Where do you go for that kind of fellowship?

— —

Your spiritual survival in the midst of career obligations could very well depend on the quality of Christian fellowship you have. Do yourself a favor and nurture relationships with other Christians. And have fun in the process. You are a much-needed soldier in the Lord's army, but you won't be much good if you try to win the battle alone. Live it up in the Lord!

# Out from Under the Bushel

—　—

*In the same way, let your light shine before men,*
*that they may see your good deeds and praise your*
*Father in heaven.*

AS A YOUNGSTER IN Sunday school I used to sing "This
Little Light of Mine," that catchy little tune about making
sure our lights shine for Christ. It's a great song with more
meaning than I ever realized back then, because in the
business world especially, those of us who are Christians
seem to blend into the scenery. We've become almost invisible. Ask yourself, how many of your colleagues know
you are a Christian? We may have succeeded in our fields
of endeavor, but few of our non-Christian colleagues know
we are believers. That's kind of sad when you realize that
even in the major-league world of television, academia,
business, and philanthropy, there are lots of solid, dedicated Christians. Maybe this personal story will illustrate
my point.

A few months ago, my wife and I received an invitation
to join other "Christian leaders" and their spouses at a
wonderful resort in the intermountain West for three days
of fellowship, prayer, and study on the topic of "character
necessary for leadership." We certainly did not consider
ourselves Christian leaders, and we didn't know any of the

other couples who had been invited, but we trusted the friend who had given us the invitation and figured the worst that could happen would be that we would have three days in some of the most beautiful country God had created on the North American continent.

As it turned out, we were so dazzled by our fellow invitees that even the glories of the magnificent Rockies paled. Our companions for the three days included a former White House Chief of Staff, the dean of a prestigious midwestern law school, the chairman emeritus of one of the country's most famous corporations, a philosophy professor from a PAC 10 school, a key executive of an internationally-known forest products company, a brilliant scholar associated with a Washington think tank, and several other business and intellectual luminaries.

We found these people deeply committed to Jesus Christ, immersed in God's Word, and actively, if quietly, working to build the kingdom. We were blown away by the spiritual quality of our time together, by the scriptural insights we gained through sharing with them, and by the very meaningful sessions of prayer we enjoyed together. The three days were a thrilling, never-to-be-forgotten interlude. My wife and I will never be quite the same after those days with those people in that magnificent setting.

Our final session together was to be a time when everyone would share. As my turn approached, I was surprised that a general feeling of sadness was almost overwhelming me. As I tried to analyze this sadness and understand why it was gripping me so, my thoughts slowly sorted themselves out. I was sad because I suddenly realized that so very few people in America knew there existed Christians such as the ones gathered with me in that beautiful room in the mountains.

Simply put, most Americans—Christians and non-Christians—just don't realize how many Bible-believing, God-honoring Christians are in positions of influence and leadership. Most non-Christians see only the caricatures—the failed television evangelists, the flamboyant preachers, the ultra right-wing zealots. They rarely see our best thinkers, writers, artists, musicians, actors, and business-men. Healthy, dynamic Christians—our most compelling witnesses—have become invisible. And you know what? It's our own fault. We've been so busy trying to make it in our respective fields that we've set our belief system aside, perhaps fearful that faith and the real world can't mix. And when we finally decide to do something about our faith, it is usually an awkward attempt to convert someone who doesn't know what he's converting to and therefore doesn't want anything to do with it.

You and I need to begin right now to change that per-ception. Those of us who care, who take seriously the scriptural admonition to be salt, must begin now to enter the fray (we are in a daily spiritual battle) at the level of our abilities and hope that others with more talent will follow. This means that we will have to make sure we are highly visible as we hold up the Savior and point men and women to Him. Those of us who have achieved some standing in business or other endeavors must begin more consciously, more regularly, and more openly to use whatever platform we have to tell who Christ is, why He came, and what this means to Americans late in the twentieth century.

How can we do that? How can we be open and public about our faith without turning people off and thereby losing our influence? Let me answer first by suggesting a few things to avoid:

- Avoid highly visible involvement in boycotts and protests. First, I don't think such actions do much good, nor do they offer a compelling witness to our non-Christian colleagues. Second, you could lose your job over such activity. Public-relations-minded businesses do not take kindly to their employees becoming involved in controversial activities. What have you gained by getting fired over picketing an abortion clinic? Now don't get me wrong. There may be times when you must stand firmly by your principles, even if it means losing your job. But going out of your way to attract attention to your political views just doesn't make sense—unless, of course, you're a politician.

- Don't force your beliefs on subordinates (or anyone, for that matter). It may be tempting to use your position of authority to force an employee to sit through your discourse on why he needs Jesus, but it just isn't fair. Put yourself in the other guy's shoes. If your boss happened to be a Muslim, would you like it if he made you listen to his profession of faith in Allah and the teachings of the Koran?

- Don't steer every conversation toward religion. Again, this turns more people off than on, and brands you as someone to stay away from. Your well-intentioned effort to promote the gospel will actually cause you to have less influence on others.

These and other tactics are intrusive and will eventually alienate the very people you hope to influence. Whenever a young Christian executive asks me how to become more visible with his faith in the workplace, I always advise, "Be yourself, be natural, and be ready when God sends you opportunities to speak a word or commit a kind deed on His behalf." In sports management and television production, we often say it's the little things that count: a follow-up thank-you note after a meeting, remembering names, showing up on time, etc. Well, it's the same thing when it comes to representing our Lord in the marketplace. Be kind and considerate to every client and colleague. Develop an interest in them as people. Be understanding and concerned when you learn of misfortune they have experienced. Be the one in your office who is known to have a heart for people, who has time to listen to a problem.

How will these little things help you become more visible as a Christian? By showing a Christlike attitude, I guarantee you will soon begin getting questions like the one I get now and then from people who really don't know me very well: "You know Bob, there's something about you that makes me think you're one of those guys that goes to church and reads the Bible a lot. Are you?" What an opening—and I didn't even have to hammer him over the head with a Bible. All I did—which is really very little and enormously easy—is live out my beliefs.

To gain recognition as a Christian in the marketplace, you must earn it, not demand it. Too many times we either keep our faith in the suitcase, unpacking it only in the hotel room and then when we get back home. Or, to the other extreme, we make a big deal about praying before we eat or nailing someone at the coffee machine with a well-rehearsed sermonette. Neither option works very well. Instead of working so hard to let people know you're a Christian, ease up a bit and simply live out the gospel, depending on the Holy Spirit to strengthen you and God's grace to forgive you when you don't quite measure up.

Beyond the little things, there are some other ways for you to become more visible as a Christian in your work world. Here are just a few that will gradually and naturally identify you as a Christian:

- Become active in a local church. Be up front with your colleagues and clients if you need to reschedule meetings that conflict with important church meetings, just as someone else might say, "Gee, I can't make it because I agreed to help out with a Rotary Club benefit."
- Include colleagues in your entertainment plans when you would normally only invite Christian friends to a party. Give your "happy pagans" a peek at some healthy Christians.
- Invite your pastor to stop by your office and give him a tour of the building or ask him to join you for an informal lunch with some of your office buddies. Treat him as a professional, which he is.

- Share quality Christian literature with colleagues or clients. Be careful here because the temptation is to hand them a book on sin or salvation and hope the book will convert them. Instead, use inspirational biographies of prominent public figures like former baseball star Dave Dravecky (*Comeback*) or loan a copy of a magazine like *Marriage Partnership* (465 Gundersen, Carol Stream, IL 60187).
- Support a Christian charity or Christian college. When appropriate, introduce that organization to a close friend from work. Let him see the good work that is done through Christian organizations, and for goodness sakes, don't hit him up for a donation!
- If there's a serious illness or death in the family of one of your colleagues, send a note or card that says, "I'm thinking of you. You're in my prayers."

All of these activities fit naturally into anyone's life. You would expect similar treatment from anyone else in your circle of associates. These things are legitimate activities that are a part of who and what you are, not "pre-evangelism" designed to sneak up on unsuspecting "prospects." And it's only natural to share these interests and activities with those you rub shoulders with in your career. Be sensitive about following these activities up with a pointed invitation to come to church or a heart-to-heart talk about where your friends will spend eternity. I recall the betrayal I once felt when someone invited me to his house for a social gathering, only to discover it was an attempt to sell us all on an investment opportunity. The gospel doesn't need to be camouflaged, just lived out naturally in your everyday life.

Finally, if you make your faith a normal extension of your everyday life and are sensitive about not trying to hammer your friends into the kingdom, I'm convinced you will have opportunities to explain your beliefs to your unsaved friends and colleagues. It may not happen on your timetable—it will probably occur at a time that is most inconvenient, like maybe in the middle of the night during a friend's time of crisis. But if you let your light shine properly, eventually it will attract interest. Be ready.

—  —

I long for the day when our love for God is so great that all Christians will become winsome public witnesses to His love for mankind as we go about our work. You are not alone; you are part of a grand movement of Christians that began when our Lord gave us our marching orders. You may pray regularly for missionaries, but never forget that you, too, have been placed right in the middle of a great and glorious mission field. Don't hide His light under a bushel. Don't snuff it out with overzealousness and insensitivity to the needs of your colleagues. Be yourself. Let your life be a "Nike advertisement" for the kingdom of God.

# When Everyone Is
# Fooling Around But You

——

*Marriage should be honored by all, and the marriage
bed kept pure, for God will judge the adulterer and
all the sexually immoral.*

Hebrews 13:4

For most of two weeks we had been closeted in a huge
New York hotel, spending our days and much of our nights
in rancorous, contentious negotiations with millions of dollars at stake. When there is a great deal of money on the
table, the tigers prowl and nothing is easy. These particular negotiations were even more complicated because they
brought together interests from all parts of the world with all
the baggage of cultural differences, nationalism, and racial
and ethnic mistrust. Even more difficult was the fact that
every gain for one party was automatically a loss for some
other group. There were almost no win/win situations.

After the last session, I was drained, still tense, and felt
almost physically beaten up. My business associate, who is
also a Christian, stopped by my suite to chat, nurse our
wounds, and celebrate any victories we may have won.
After a while he looked me square in the eye and said,
"Do you realize that everyone else from those meetings is
out getting laid? That's how they unwind, while we sit

here in your hotel room and maybe order a snack from room service. Sometimes I can't help but envy those guys."

— —

Let's face it, if you're a business traveler, one of the easiest things to do is cheat on your wife. To "get laid," to use the more sanitized version from the world's vocabulary. It's one of the "perks" that come with success. Sex on the road behind your wife's back is as available as room service; in some cultures, it's offered just as we might arrange to have a basket of fruit sent up to a client's hotel room. And you don't have to look like Tom Cruise to be approached. Believe me, I know.

Despite being a fifty-plus, overweight, physically un-attractive, and usually tired-looking businessman, I get hit up now and then. No kidding.

Once, I had the honor of introducing my good friend, tennis great Jack Kramer, at a very chic charity fundraiser. It was held at one of Chicago's major museums. After say-ing a few words about Jack, I walked away from the podium and took my seat. Almost before Jack began to speak, a very attractive young woman came up to me, kissed me on the cheek, and said, "You were wonderful."

Wow!

Quickly, I regained my composure and sort of mum-bled thank you. Later that evening as I walked out of the banquet hall, that same young woman fell in step beside me, put her arm on mine, and said, "I'm on the charity committee (I'll say!). I know you have a suite over at the

Ritz-Carlton, so let's you and I go over there and make a night of it."

Pow!

Out of the absolute blue this old guy was being offered something both tempting and frightening. Talk about being discombobulated. Something inside of me said yes, but my response was, "Um, I'm . . . ah . . . well, ah . . . sorry, but I don't think so."

Not to be denied, the young lady said she was sorry too but that if I changed my mind to give her a call at a number she had written on a piece of paper and placed in my hand. "I'll be there all night," she purred as she walked off toward the parking lot.

I headed the opposite direction, grabbed a cab, rushed back to my hotel room, double-locked the door, and called down to the front desk to tell them I would not be accepting any calls that evening. The last thing I wanted was a phone call saying, "I'm in the lobby, may I come up?"

As I said, I'm far from your basic hunk. I share this anecdote not to brag, but to underscore the fact that no one is immune to this sort of thing. In my case, I suspect the young lady thought anyone involved with professional sports is loaded. I've been told by my well-heeled (and equally ugly) friends that they are frequent targets of unscrupulous women who would like nothing more than to trap a guy and maybe make a few bucks in the process.

Then there was the case a couple of years ago involving a National League umpire who took a woman up to his room for a night of pleasure. She had approached him in the hotel bar (another good reason to stay out of bars) and one thing led to another. You know, boys will be boys, especially with girls. Well this boy grew up real fast because his little rendezvous cost him about $15,000 in cash along with his Rolex. It seems the girl slipped something into his drink, he passed out, and she made off with the loot. Oldest trick in the book, but it still happens.

You might think that the fact you go to church and are happily married will protect you from yielding to temptation on the road. True, a strong marriage does go a long way toward keeping you from fooling around, but once you begin to think you're invincible, temptation has a way of working its magic charms on you. The fact is, unless you are prepared, you have the two proverbial chances of standing up to sexual temptation: slim and none. To paraphrase, "Eternal vigilance is the price of purity." One senior pastor, a good friend, was so shaken by the news of the fall of once-respected colleagues that he has instituted a daily ritual with one of his associate pastors. Each day they face each other privately and ask two questions: "Are your hands clean? Are your eyes clean?"

Does this sound extreme? If it does, you do not fully recognize the danger. No one is immune. And part of the reason we are so vulnerable is that we are constantly bombarded by two powerful messages. The first says, "If you're not getting yours, you're the only one. Everyone else out there is having fun. You're missing out. What a nerd!"

Nonsense! Not everyone is doing it. In spite of the tremendous sexual looseness of our times, many men, many businessmen, many traveling businessmen have determined to remain pure, to honor their marriage vows to the fullest and to obey the Bible. All they're "missing" is the tremendous guilt, self-loathing, family brokenness, and shame that comes with a promiscuous lifestyle. Just ask Magic Johnson what you're missing when you don't shack up with everyone who's available.

The second message is even more potent. It's the "no harm, no foul" pitch. You're in a city a thousand miles from home. You are presented with a willing partner, a consenting adult. No one will ever know.

Again, this is a lie that the Enemy wants you to believe. The person you harm the most may be yourself, but your wife, your family, your partner, and her loved ones will also suffer. Deep in your heart you will know you've broken a sacred vow. Things will never be the same between you and your wife, even if she never knows, or even if she learns and forgives you. You will know, and that will make all the difference. Are you prepared to live with that awful knowledge just for a few minutes of sexual pleasure?

Believe me, turning down an evening with that young, beautiful woman wasn't easy. I'd be lying if I told you I didn't at least give her offer a passing thought. But over the years I've learned some things I can do to protect myself from this sort of powerful temptation. Maybe they will work for you, too:

- Call your wife every night.
- Keep her picture with you and look at it at the end of your work day.
- Stay out of bars.
- Don't flirt.

- Keep your hands to yourself; avoid "innocent" hugs and touches.
- Include your wife and family in conversations.
- Avoid pornography or suggestive movies.
- Watch the movie, "Fatal Attraction."

That last one may need some explaining, because it is the kind of movie I would generally tell Christians to avoid. There's a lot of rough language and some very steamy sex scenes. But the overall effect it has on most men who watch it is to make them never want to have an affair. The price the star, Michael Douglas, pays for his one-night stand is absolutely horrible. Maybe you don't really need to watch the movie—just think of what it would be like if your illicit amour decided to stalk you and your family.

Let me also add that working to strengthen your marriage is still the best antidote to temptation. If you are in love with your wife, your head won't turn as readily when someone walks by. Don't become married to your work. When you're home, carve out special times with your wife. If your relationship is strained, don't hesitate to seek counseling. You will be less likely to blow it on the road if you've built and nurtured a strong relationship with your wife. As a friend of mine likes to say, "Who needs hamburger on the road when you can get prime rib at home?"

━ ━

The Bible tells us to flee immorality. Flee is an active verb. It means to run, to get out of there. Stay awake. Stay alert. Don't get trapped. The pure and honest relationship you have with your wife is a precious gift to be protected.

Few things on earth rival the feeling of returning home from a business trip and being able to hug your wife with a clear conscience.

Sexual purity. As we used to say to the pitcher who's leading going into the ninth inning, "It's yours to lose."

# Secretaries: A Dangerous Blessing

*It is God's will that you should be sanctified: that you should avoid sexual immorality; that each of you should learn to control his own body in a way that is holy and honorable.*

1 THESSALONIANS 4:3–4

FOR FORTY OR MORE hours a week, she's right at your side. You joke with her, confide in her, and celebrate small victories with her. Sometimes you have to push her to meet a deadline, and if you're a decent guy, you reward her when the job is done. You know her strengths and weaknesses, and she likely knows yours as well.

Before long, you find it easy to talk with her about some personal issues in your life. Maybe even the fact that you and your wife are having some problems. She seems so understanding. So dedicated. So loyal. You love the way she shields you from intrusions and covers for you when you forgot an important appointment. It's almost as if she's more than a secretary.

At that point, she is, and that's dangerous!

No business relationship is closer than that of a manager and his private secretary. Under the best of circumstances, no business relationship is more positive and productive. A great secretary can literally make her boss at least twice as effective as he would be alone. Dollar for dollar, a terrific secretary is the best personnel buy a businessman can make. A first-class secretary is a great blessing. And yet, the closeness of the relationship, the amount of time spent together, and the nature of the relationship present real dangers for the spiritual well-being of both parties—dangers that extend to the homes and families of each.

The boss/secretary affair is so commonplace it is almost a cliché. The second wife of a successful businessman is more likely to have been his secretary than any other person, and in those cases, the second marriage is almost always preceded by a clandestine affair of some duration and which resulted in at least one broken home and sometimes two.

As we all know, Christians are not immune to these kinds of dangers. I know of one tragic situation in which the president of a Christian college abandoned his career in Christian higher education, and even more distressingly, his wife and children, to take off with his secretary. As they say, it happens in the "best" of families.

It seems the more productive the relationship between an executive and his secretary, the greater the peril. The closer they get in business, the more triumphs and defeats they share, the more they know about each other, the more they can accomplish together. But, as these things increase, so does the danger.

A secretary often sees the man for whom she works as powerful, authoritative, and somehow more glamorous than other men of her acquaintance. He is almost always more affluent.

The executive sees his secretary as a loyal person who is adept at making life easier for him, someone who "understands" him better than anyone else (certainly better than his wife at home who wants him to take out the garbage, spend more time with the children, and paint the trim on the house). She is almost always younger and more physically attractive than his wife. A great-looking secretary who, by the nature of her job almost always says yes to her boss's every request, is a huge temptation for any man.

With all these inherent dangers, is it possible for a Christian businessman to have the business advantages of a dynamic secretary without succumbing to the obvious temptations? Of course it is, and many wholesome relationships exist between Christian *and* non-Christian executives and their secretaries. But almost never by accident. It takes vigilance and self-discipline.

As with any potential peril, the best defense is in knowing just how dangerous the relationship with your secretary can be. I worry most about guys who say, "I never worry about it." They should. And you should, too, because the boss/secretary relationship, by its very nature, is emotionally charged.

Consider what happened to a close friend of mine who was just beginning his business career in a very competitive, demanding field. He was fortunate to hire as his first secretary a young lady with great skills who soon became exceptionally committed to my friend's business success. They worked very well together. But to my friend's absolute shock and amazement, she quit and stormed out of his office when he told her he was getting married. There had never been any kind of romantic involvement between the two, but the business relationship was so close and intense that the secretary felt somehow betrayed by the fact that another woman was in the way. (The happy conclusion to this story is that my friend did indeed marry his fiancée and now they share the joy of twin daughters twenty-one years old who are graduating from Yale. *And* he talked his secretary into coming back after a healthy but frank conversation about his and her expectations. She still works for him, twenty-three years later.)

The moral of the story: Understand the intensity of the relationship from the beginning and channel it into good things.

Another helpful approach to this problem is to let your secretary know that you are a Christian and are committed to a Christian lifestyle. This kind of declaration provides an ongoing deterrent for both of you. In this age of "political correctness," however, it is important that the announcement of your faith be done with tact and sensitivity (it always should be done this way!) and should not be seen by your secretary as a religious test for her or as coercion of any kind to convert to your faith.

Although it is not always possible, I have found it to be very healthy for my secretary and my wife to know each other and, when possible, to become friends. It doesn't hurt for your secretary to also know your children well. This is just another strong two-way barrier to untoward behavior.

A good secretary is privy to many confidences, from your salary to your medical condition, but never get in the habit of sharing confidences with your secretary that you would not share with your wife. And never ask your secretary to cover for you where your wife is concerned. It might seem harmless to say, "Don't tell Marty I'm taking the afternoon off to play golf," but it is the first step to disaster. For one thing, it violates the trust you have with your wife, and it also gives your secretary a signal that she's trusted more than your wife is.

Of all the dangers in the boss/secretary relationship, none is more perilous than traveling together. It is easy to rationalize taking a secretary on a trip with you: "Just think of all the work we can get done on the plane." "She can type up the corrected contract while we are there, and we can get it signed before we come back." "Without the distractions of the office, we can really concentrate on putting a great proposal together." "She's really been working hard and deserves a trip out of town." "She's never been to New York." And so on.

Forget it! None of the positives outweigh the negatives. Start with the biblical admonition to avoid the very appearance of evil. Once you head to the airport with your secretary, everyone from people in accounting to those who clean your offices will assume the worst. Also, traveling together, you naturally stay in the same hotel, and will probably have dinner together, and soon the temptation quotient goes off the charts. For good reason the Bible tells us to "flee from youthful lusts and pursue righteousness."

My secretary has been with me for many years and is one of the best. Even though the business we are in requires a very heavy travel schedule for me, she has only

ever taken *one* business trip and that was because we were
doing a television interview with President Reagan and I
wanted her to have the opportunity to meet him. However,
if a number of our other colleagues had not also been in the
same traveling group, she would not have made the trip.
President or no president, the two of us would never have
traveled alone.

As I said, my secretary has been with me for a number
of years. I like and appreciate her tremendously, and yet,
even these days when everyone seems to be hugging
everyone else, I never hug her. I never touch her. Many of
my business colleagues put an arm around their secretaries
as a matter of course. Many routinely give their secretaries
a little hug when departing for or returning from a trip.
Maybe that's okay, but I would rather take the coward's
way out. The way I look at it, "discretion is the better part
of valor."

Common sense dictates other helpful cautions:

- Avoid closed-door sessions where only you and your
  secretary are present.
- Keep the relationship professional, with a minimum
  of joking and teasing.
- You are your secretary's employer, not her counselor.
  Don't encourage conversation about her marriage or
  other personal issues.
- Never, ever, ever share an off-color or suggestive
  joke or comment.
- If you have even a slight hint that she may view you
  as more than a boss, go directly to your personnel director or another colleague and share your concerns.

—  —

The world treats secretary/boss affairs as an occupa-
tional hazard. Your faith teaches that any adulterous relationship is a sin. Many times, you may be caught between
the two views. Go with your faith. Be alert. Be professional.
Set a higher standard of behavior in your office. And when
you catch yourself mentally stepping over the line, repent
and seek God's forgiveness. As a man of God, you must
protect your family by keeping the relationship between
you and your secretary pure and without blame.

# You'll Be Hearing from My Lawyer

*Settle matters quickly with your adversary who is taking you to court.*

MATTHEW 5:25

RECENTLY, I WAS IN Hong Kong having breakfast with a former U.S. congressman, who now has many years of experience as an international businessman. While we were eating, a Chinese attorney came up to our table and served legal papers on my friend. It was not a serious suit, almost a frivolous one, but it certainly spoiled the day for my friend in spite of his sophistication and experience. He took it very seriously, as well he should. Even the simplest of lawsuits can consume thousands of dollars and hundreds of hours that most businessmen can ill afford to lose.

Have you been sued yet? If not, the chances are that if you are in business, it will not be too long before the litigiousness of the times catches up with you. These days in America it seems almost everyone is constantly suing everyone else. As Christians, how are we to react to lawsuits? What should our response be to being sued?

Having been sued several times, I can tell you that almost nothing focuses the mind like being personally named in a lawsuit that demands you pay a huge sum of money to someone claiming to have been wronged. It is a rare person who sees a lawsuit against them as just another day at the office. As Ray Miller writing in "Fellowship Report" said, "Remember that, regardless of how tough you feel or how strong your witness, being on the wrong end of a big lawsuit doesn't feel good. . . . Many of us who have had the same experience surely must have said: What do I do now, God?" Good question.

Regardless of the merits of a suit against you, you know that it will be expensive in terms of time, money, and emotional energy. You know it will be debilitating and frustrating. Again, how should a Christian respond?

One of the worst and least productive years of my life and the lives of many of my colleagues and friends came when Jimmy Connors, then a very young tennis player, sued us for several million dollars in an antitrust action. While all the legal nuances were quite complex, the basic suit was quite simple. Jimmy (really his attorneys and advisors) felt he should be able to have all the benefits of what was then the new Association of Tennis Professionals, without having to join the association. Those of us who had formed the ATP—people such as Arthur Ashe, Jack Kramer, John Newcombe, Stan Smith, and virtually every other leading player in the world—felt that Jimmy should join the association in order to get its benefits.

That seemingly simple lawsuit dominated our lives for an entire year, cost more than a million dollars in legal fees, brought the development of the sport of professional tennis to a virtual standstill, and really solved nothing. The suit was eventually settled with no real winner (except perhaps the lawyers) and with many ambiguities remaining.

And this suit, as they almost all do, had many personal implications as well. Some people never got over it and have never forgiven those on the opposite side. Some have now gone to their respective graves harboring ill feelings. Great tennis players whose playing careers are winding down, and who should be delighting in each other's company and reminiscing about memorable matches and historic tournaments, are still alienated because of the suit. Lawsuits are expensive in more ways than just money. Christians need to remember this.

Lawsuits these days can also leave Christians in a quandary when what seem to be sound business practices run head on into moral imperatives. Our company has been representing professional athletes for almost twenty-five years. We have always offered all the traditional services of a large sports management company, including contract negotiation, legal advice (we have a number of in-house attorneys), marketing services, and investment counseling. Recently, we were faced with a lawsuit from a former client, an athlete who had not been active for several years. His suit did not allege any misappropriation of funds, nor did he claim he lost any money following our company's investment advice. He was suing because his investments had not made as much as he hoped they would make!

We settled the case rather than try it in court, even though we knew we had done nothing wrong. It would have been expensive and time consuming to fight. The publicity in the sports world, the arena in which we work, would have been negative even if we had won the suit. Headlines saying, "Former Star Athlete Sues His Management Firm" are remembered long after the small story several months later which tells of the final outcome of the case. Yes, it seemed to be good business to settle, but was it the moral, the Christian thing to do? Was it honest to, in a sense, declare defeat when in our hearts we knew we were right?

Before getting into specifics, my bottom-line advice is to make sure you maintain a close, personal walk with God through any period of legal action. It is too easy to let your emotions govern your actions as you get caught up in the issues of a particular case. While it may not be business as usual in your office, it must be business as usual where your faith is concerned. And believe me, there will be times when you feel as if everyone is against you, which makes it all the more important to have that strong relationship with the Lord.

There may be a time when a lawsuit will hit with such force and be so all-consuming that it will threaten to sweep aside even your most basic beliefs. At that point it may be terribly tempting to say, in effect, "I am a Christian and I believe the Bible and all that, but this is business. This is survival." The world's reaction to a lawsuit is to hire a "take no prisoners—go for the jugular—legal gunslinger" and stick it to them. But if your faith has any validity, if you really believe in the life-changing message of the gospel and that your treasure is in heaven and not on earth, you cannot approach a lawsuit this way. Suspending your biblically-based belief system just because you're in a lawsuit is not an option.

So the foundational principal for Christians involved in a lawsuit is to make sure you remain grounded in your faith. Basic Christian disciplines such as praying, reading the Bible, going to church, and meditating will be extremely helpful to you during this stressful period. They will liberate you from fear, reduce passion, and be a good check on your attitude.

It would be extremely naive of me, however, to tell you to just pray and everything will be okay. You can pray all day and still lose your shirt. I firmly believe God expects us to use every resource to protect ourselves from unwarranted civil action. More specifically, seek godly counsel whenever you are involved in a lawsuit. Believe it or not, the term "godly attorney" is not an oxymoron. More and more Christians see the law as an area of service and base their practices on biblical principles. Most cities have a Christian Legal Society or similar organization which can refer you to Christian attorneys who practice in areas of the law relevant to your particular need. Your pastor or the pastors of other churches should also be able to direct you to a Christian attorney.

One word of caution, however. The primary criterion for hiring an attorney ought to be competence. Just because an attorney is a Christian does not mean he or she is a good lawyer. I remember hearing someone talking about the advantages of having a physician who was a Christian and the response was, "I don't care if the surgeon is Christian or not—I just want to make sure he knows what he's doing."

Regardless of who your attorney is, make it very clear that you want all legal procedures carried out in harmony with biblical principles. In general, that means you are interested in fairness and justice, not vengeance or retribution. It also means you will not stand for any kind of deception, even if it may technically be legal.

What if you are the party who has been wronged? Are Christians ever justified in bringing suits of their own to redress wrongs? As this is being written, the company of which I am a director is suing the National Basketball Association and its commissioner, David Stern. David is one of the men in sports I admire most, and has been a good friend. Forget the merits of the suit; this is not a happy state of affairs. What is my obligation to my company, vis-à-vis my obligation to my friend? What is my obligation as a Christian?

God's word has been helpful to me in terms of how to redress a wrong. Matthew 18 offers very clear step-by-step directions on how you should proceed from an initial, private face-to-face meeting with the offending party all the way through mediation and arbitration. Although these instructions are specifically aimed at believers who are in conflict with each other, the principles are worth following. The basic idea is to first try to resolve the issue on a personal level, and if that fails, to bring in outside assistance.

I also strongly recommend that you attempt to settle your dispute through mediation rather than through legal action. The whole purpose of mediation is to allow an objective, neutral party to work with the disputing parties to find a settlement. It just makes good sense to do this. More and more businesses are seeking the help of an arbitrator to settle disputes. Again, the Christian Legal Society (2851 Meadowview Road, Falls Church, Virginia, 22042) is a source of solid help as you deal with legal concerns in a biblical way.

Finally, err on the side of keeping the peace. Romans 12:18 says, "If possible, so far as it depends on you, live at peace with everyone." I have been associated in business with people who seek strife, who are not happy unless there is current controversy, and who will generate dispute if none arises naturally. That kind of attitude is antithetical to God's way for us. We should see peace as a goal and strive for it. That doesn't mean Christians should be passive, rolling over anytime someone comes along with a lawsuit—we need to be firm in our convictions and fight fairly and diligently to defend ourselves. But this admonition from Romans refers more to the attitude with which we approach others. I admire those rare individuals who can be embroiled in a legal action, yet maintain a beautiful sense of calm and dignity. Ideally, you should come out of a lawsuit with your head high and the knowledge that in every step of the process you reflected the spirit of Christ. I can't say I've done that all the time, but it is a goal I always try to maintain.

━ ━

The business world is an arena where power and strength are the weapons of choice. Enter that arena unarmed and you'll be pummeled from every direction. Fortunately, Christians were never called to be weak or wimpy. The power of truth, fairness, justice, and mercy will prevail against even the craftiest opponent who tries to pervert the legal system to his advantage.

If someone wrongs you and legal action seems necessary, fight strongly and fairly with the power that comes with righteousness. Honor God through every step, and He will honor you. And if you are served papers for something you have done, tap into that same source of power. Regardless of the outcome in terms of our country's legal system, you will emerge a true winner. You will sleep soundly at night and be able to face the next day with the confidence that comes from obeying God.

# When AIDS Strikes

——

*Death has climbed in through our windows and has entered our fortresses; it has cut off the children from the streets and the young men from the public squares.*

IF YOU HAVE NOT prepared for AIDS in your business, you had better start today. Regardless of the size of your company or if you are self-employed, I guarantee you will one day look into the eyes of a friend or colleague or associate who has AIDS. We have already had two AIDS-related deaths in our company, and my friend and client, Arthur Ashe, passed away last year with complications from AIDS. Through these deaths, the reality of the world, its problems, and its diseases crashed into our consciousness. Where we once sort of took life for granted, we don't anymore. We've gotten our wake-up call, a rude reminder that even though our company is made up mostly of Christians, we are not immune from this terrible disease.

What do *you* think of AIDS? How would you respond if a client or colleague contracted the disease? Would you be uncomfortable having a person with AIDS work closely with you? What about your company's insurance with relation to employees with AIDS? Will they get adequate care, especially as the disease drags on? As a Christian, do you believe your company's policies towards AIDS sufferers is fair?

Tough questions, indeed, but ones you had better begin thinking about and perhaps discussing with your colleagues. When AIDS struck our company, I'd like to say that the way we responded was the result of careful and strategic planning, but it wasn't. We knew hardly anything about the disease; we didn't even know what questions to ask. And maybe that was the way God wanted it, because a key leader in our company responded to AIDS in a way that could only be described as Christlike.

━ ━

When AIDS first struck our company, it hit a longtime colleague, someone with whom both Dennis Spenser, my associate, and I had worked for many years. This was in the very early days of the epedemic when we knew even less about the disease than we know now, especially about the way it could be contracted.

Despite concern for his own health and that of his wife and children, Dennis, a professional with tremendous responsibility in the company, put almost everything else aside to minister to our friend. With courage and compassion, he became a spiritual counselor and made absolutely certain that the truths of the Bible were available to our stricken associate.

Many of us would have stopped there, for I've observed that Christians are big on introducing people to Christ but small on following through on their physical needs. Not Dennis. As the ravages of the disease became more pronounced, Dennis undertook many of the physical tasks—many unpleasant and even frightening—necessary in the care of a dying AIDS patient. When our friend could no longer drive, Dennis did his shopping and chauffered him to his many doctor's appointments. He even took on the responsibility of guarding our friend's property from erstwhile friends who felt entitled to his belongings.

This went on for several weeks. During this time, Dennis was also the main point of contact with our friend's family who lived far away and was, naturally, bewildered and frightened. He became a counselor and source of strength for them as well.

Even after dementia took over and robbed our colleague of conscious thought and dignity, Dennis stayed with him. When death finally and mercifully came, Dennis continued to minister, handling funeral arrangements, hosting grieving relatives, and winding up all the legal affairs.

Calling Dennis a Good Samaritan is not enough. In my mind, he went beyond the Samaritan and set a new and higher standard of how Christ's love is to be made real in even the most difficult of life's circumstances.

I'd like to think our company learned from Dennis's example because, when AIDS hit us again, the corporate response went far beyond what is generally required or expected in today's business environment. My partner, Donald Dell, made it clear from the start that the company would take care of its fallen comrade. There was never any question but that all our corporate resources would be available in the fight against the disease. It cost us tens of thousands of dollars and our friend still died a terrible death. Still, we have the comfort of knowing that we did all we could do, that we did not look for or take an easy, less expensive, or "corporately prudent" way out. I hope we will always have this kind of courage.

What about you? Would you be willing to step in like Dennis did and live out your faith through caring for what is fast becoming the twentieth-century equivalent of the leper? Can you influence your company to evaluate its policy for dealing with AIDS? This is really what it means to be salt and light in a morally decaying and darkened world.

You know, it's awfully hard to claim the scriptural promise that "all things work together for good" when confronted with the gruesome process of death from AIDS. Our neatly tied theologies pale when you're sitting on the edge of a man's bed while he's retching. "God has a plan for your life" seems almost like a curse in times like these. You will be of little help to a person with AIDS if all you can do is remain at the superficial level. What is needed is what often is so hard to give: your time, your honesty, your presence.

When the tough times come, when life's most tragic circumstances hit very close to home, we must be sure to put our theoretical faith into concrete action. In the foul-smelling apartment of a dying AIDS victim, sunlight does not stream through stained glass, no organ music is heard, no choirs sing—it is dark and frightening. The Christ of the Garden and of the Cross needs to become very real to that person whose decision for eternity may be based on your response to him.

—— ——

Don't wait until AIDS intrudes into your comfort zone. Begin now to think through your response to a colleague or client who contracts AIDS. Ask your boss if you could form a special committee to look into ways of responding to AIDS. Learn as much as you can about the disease. Allow the Holy Spirit to replace your fear with a spirit of love and compassion. You could very well be the one God has chosen "before the foundations of the earth were set" to be a modern-day Samaritan to an employee or client with AIDS. That's not a burden, but a great privilege!

# A Handshake That Can Be Trusted

*A good name is more desirable than great riches.*

PROVERBS 22:1

IN MY TENURE IN professional athletics I've met a lot of interesting people. You might think the athletes have had the most impact on me, but more often it's the people behind the scenes. I'd like to tell you a little story about one of those people who, in my opinion, did something that few men are willing to do: turn down millions of dollars in order to keep a promise. I was a firsthand witness and a minor participant in this inspiring story, and count his example among the richest blessings God has given me.

— —

David F. Dixon wanted an NFL team. For Dave, it would be a business and an asset for New Orleans, his hometown and a city he dearly loves. Dave was not wealthy by NFL ownership standards, but he believed in his dream and set out on an amazing journey to reach it.

During the 1960s, television and skillful management were beginning to make the NFL the sports and business juggernaut it has now become. When the original cities in the league were being joined by new owners in new, ambitious cities, Dave Dixon began to dream of acquiring an

NFL franchise for New Orleans. He had some very formidable obstacles to overcome.

New Orleans is colorful, fascinating, and a very special American city. It is not, however, a wealthy one. Of even more concern to any sports organization is how low it ranks as a television market among U.S. cities. To be a lucrative franchise, you need to be in a city with a big television market, and New Orleans could not offer that.

In addition to economic realities, there were other obstacles. While always more liberal than many other cities in the South, New Orleans had its share of racial problems. Dave needed to convince the grand poobahs of the NFL that New Orleans would present no more racial issues to the league than would any other American city.

By using studies by prestigious research firms, selling his own economic growth projections, and personally integrating some of the South's most famous restaurants and hotels, Dave knocked down those obstacles one by one. But the battle, it turned out, was just heating up.

It became clear that to win in this high-stakes game Dave needed Washington muscle. In dealing with the ever-politically sensitive NFL, Capitol Hill leverage would be a necessary tool. Dave went after and got the two strongest Louisiana players inside the Beltway. If the NFL was going to deny New Orleans the right to play in its league, they would have to look deep into the eyes of Representative Hale Boggs in the U.S. House of Representatives and Senator Russell Long.

Pete Rozelle, the astute and powerful NFL commissioner, needed a very compelling rationale for denying

New Orleans a franchise before taking on the likes of
Congressman Boggs and Senator Long, and the stadium
situation in New Orleans presented him with just such a rationale. Dave assumed he could use the venerable Sugar
Bowl stadium owned by Tulane University, but the school's
officials decided to tear it down. No stadium, no team, no
NFL franchise.

For most people that would have been the end of a
dream. But in only a matter of days, Dave Dixon became
convinced that the stadium situation presented an opportunity of gigantic proportions. Why not build a great new
stadium, a domed stadium, the world's greatest stadium, a
stadium whose only name could be the Superdome? For
most people, a super stadium for a poor city in a poor state
wouldn't compute. For Dave Dixon, it made perfect sense,
and it provided a sure path to that elusive NFL franchise.

Dave retained the noted and powerful Stanford
Research firm to tell him both how to build a supercolos-
sal domed stadium in downtown New Orleans and why it
actually needed to be built for the benefit of every citizen
in New Orleans and in the state of Louisiana. From the day
that Stanford Research report reached his hands, Dave became a very formidable advocate. He would soon learn,
however, that it was a long and arduous path from having
the rationale on paper to seeing an NFL team play in a
domed stadium in downtown New Orleans.

Among one of the most important things Stanford
Research told Dave was that the only way to finance the
project was to put the full faith and credit of the state behind it. It was too big an undertaking for the city, even with

its surrounding parishes (counties) involved. It had to be a state backed effort.

So Dixon went straight to the capitol, and after presenting his case, Governor John McKeithen joined in and made it a duet. Governor McKeithen decided to risk everything, not so much on the idea of a huge stadium in New Orleans, but on a man. On David F. Dixon. In doing so, he extracted a promise from him. For his 100-percent support of the domed stadium project, the governor made Dave promise to would give 100 percent of his efforts toward the stadium until it was certain that a first-rate facility would be built. Dave gave the governor his promise without hesitation.

The highest hurdle loomed just ahead, buried in the arcane pages of the Louisiana Constitution, which would not allow the state to finance such a project. Undaunted, Dave decided it was time to change the constitution by passing a constitutional amendment, which meant holding a state-wide referendum. In typical fashion, he simply got in his car, used what money he had, and began telling every Louisianan who would listen that any self-respecting, patriotic, red-blooded, sports-loving American that was not certifiably insane would vote "yes" on an amendment that would bring the best football in the world to the best state in the union. The Cajuns, crackers, rednecks, blacks, whites, upstaters, downstaters, and everyone left over bought it, and the amendment passed.

Almost before he had time to savor the victory the first blow fell. Powerful forces in New Orleans, the ultimate "powers that be," the kind with which one does not argue

or debate, let Dave know that he would have to choose between the football team and the stadium. He could not be
involved with both due to potential conflict of interest.

Simple problem, simple solution, right? I mean, here's
a guy who all along only wanted to own an NFL team.
The stadium was only a means to an end. Besides, getting
a stadium built and operating it would be a real hassle.
Faced with the choice of owning an NFL football team or
operating a new stadium, Dave shouldn't have had to think
for a second. Except for one thing: a handshake. He had
promised the governor that no matter what happened, he
would not quit until the stadium was built. There was no
written contract, but there didn't need to be. His handshake, his word, his promise was enough.

Keeping his promise to the governor would not be easy.
The stadium and all the money it would cost was seen by
many Louisiana politicians as a huge pie to be divided up
among the power brokers in the state. With all the possi-
bilities for graft, the sharks began to circle the stadium project in ever-increasing numbers.

I had come up to New Orleans from a stint with the
Miami Dolphins to be a part of Dave's short-lived NFL
franchise administration, but stayed on to help with the stadium. Dave told me, "Bob, I intend to keep my promise to
the governor. We need to accomplish three things before
we are run out of town. We need to make sure the stadium
is built downtown where it belongs, and where it will do
the most good. We must see that we bring the nation's very
best engineers to the project. Finally, and most impor-

tantly, we must insure that the very best, most capable architects are hired."

Dave went on to say that it would take every bit of resolve we could muster to accomplish those three things and that in doing so we would expend every bit of political capital he had and we would become pariahs in the state. He also said that even with the governor working with us, even if we secured the downtown site, the best architects and engineers, that there would be no way we could keep tens of millions of dollars from being funneled through the stadium project into the pockets of the "good old boys" and their pals. He said we could go along with that nonsense and probably get rich, but he didn't have the stomach for it.

It happened just as Dave said it would. We pulled out all the stops to accomplish the three things Dave felt were necessary to keep his promise to the governor. The city would have a great stadium and an NFL team, but Dave Dixon would have neither. He would, however, have his integrity intact and his character unsullied.

You and I may not face such huge temptations to compromise our integrity, but almost everyone is constantly under pressure to cut ethical corners. There are opportunities to cheat on practically every major business deal, and I've known many good men who've compromised their integrity when those chances came their way. Even in the smaller, everyday dealings, ethics matter. Do you use your company's telephone for personal calls? Do you fudge on your travel expenses? Are you known as a man of your word?

Integrity is not something you are born with, but something you must earn. And keep. All it takes is one wrong move for your reputation to be damaged. Most of us really do know the difference between right and wrong, but it's all too easy to see the good that might come from an unethical choice. Once you begin to rationalize a particular decision that has ethical implications, you need to stop everything and ask yourself, "Am I trying to talk myself into something I know is wrong?"

I hope that every time you see the New Orleans Saints on television or read about them in the press that you will remember Dave Dixon and his integrity. I hope that every time you see an event from the Superdome you will remember his example of character. I hope that anytime in any business situation you think about shading the truth just a little, promising just a little more than you know you can deliver, or consider leaving language just a little ambiguous to provide a convenient way out, that you will remember him.

Finally, I hope all of us can begin doing a better job in the area of integrity and character. In general, Christians in business do not do any better than non-Christians in this area. In fact, too often I hear a colleague say something like, "He's one of those born-again guys, so watch out. He'll cheat you if he gets a chance." I suppose part of the problem is that we're held to a higher standard (because we claim to live up to higher standards). We need to realize that we witness more in our business transactions than we do in our public proclamations of faith.

No one rounds third and heads for home free of all regrets. You may have made some ethical errors in the past and feel pretty small compared to Dave Dixon. Maybe you need to skid to a stop and head back to third. Or maybe you've been heading in the wrong direction, but in your heart you really want to become a man of character and integrity. You can do it! Commit this day's decisions and activities to God and let Him guide you to a higher standard of honesty. Your handshake is your calling card. Keep your word. Tell the truth. It will keep you out of those exhausting squeeze plays.

# Deleting the Expletives

—▪ ▪—

*But now you must rid yourselves of all such things as these: anger, rage, malice, slander, and filthy language from your lips.*

RECENTLY, I WAS IN the New York office of a top financial executive. This guy is first-class all the way—exquisitely educated and handsomely groomed. Politically well connected, he's held an elected position and is regularly considered for cabinet-level positions when openings occur in Washington. Though we had met briefly before, this was our first in-depth meeting. I knew a fair amount about him because of his political visibility, but he knew next to nothing about me.

About the same moment I noticed two Bibles prominently displayed on his desk, he cut loose. I mean, I've heard guys swear before, but this guy let one of the worst strings of four-letter words drop as if he was deliberately trying to one-up the vilest reprobate. I'm sure he was not accustomed to such language, but just threw it in to let me know he was a good ol' boy. Frankly, it was pretty sad.

—▪ ▪—

I used to think only a certain type of people cussed: poorly educated, blue collar workers with abusive parents. But I learned really fast that foul language is not the *lingua franca* of the underprivileged. Guys in $1,000 suits who sit on powerful boards can match the profanity of any long-shoreman who has had a pallet drop on his foot. If you've been in the business or professional world for any length of time, you've probably heard every bad word you ever learned in the high school locker room . . . and more.

"Corporate cussing" presents at least two problems for the Christian professional. First, how do you respond to it without seeming like a nerd? And second, how do you avoid becoming immune to it (or picking up some unholy vocabulary along the way)? If you are unable to resolve the first problem, you'll certainly run headlong into the second. The scenario goes something like this: Your boss calls a meeting and in the course of events lets loose with more than an occasional "hell" or "damn." You'd prefer he didn't sprinkle his presentations with such profanities, but you're not sure how to talk to him about it without making him mad or making you look naive. So you keep quiet, and you know what? After a while you don't notice it. Or worse, you notice a few mild expletives creeping into your own conversations.

Now let me assure you, I don't think swearing is a sin (though I consider it a weakness). And I don't necessarily think it's the job of every Christian to become language police in their workplaces. But I do think there's a limit to what we have to take. While I have become more or less accustomed to even the vilest of language in boardrooms and executive suites, I will never be able to hear with any degree of equanimity the use of Lord's name in vain or profane ways.

So what should you do about it? How can you address the issue of profane language in your office or company? There is nothing wrong with talking privately with someone who uses profanity and admitting to that person that his language bothers you. You don't need to make a big thing about it, and you certainly shouldn't approach the person with a "holier than thou" attitude. On occasion, I have met privately with people I know fairly well and have asked them to ease up on their use of the name of Jesus Christ as a slang expression. Usually they are not even aware they have been doing it. And if you do it one-on-one, where the individual doesn't have to save face in front of his buddies, more often than not he will genuinely express his regret at offending you.

Once, in making a business presentation to a group of Coca-Cola executives in Hong Kong, my colleague and friend used the name of Jesus profanely. I saw at least one of the Coca-Cola men wince at the expletive. Discussing this with my associate privately after the meeting, I could not convince him that he had actually said what he said. Yet, I did notice he cleaned up his subsequent presentations.

If you'd like to say something, but you don't know how to do it tactfully, don't just let it go. Here are some suggestions that will give you a fair hearing when you do speak up:

- Don't try to correct those with whom you are not very close. You haven't earned the right to hold perfect strangers to your standards.
- Always deal with this issue privately. No one likes to be corrected, and we especially hate being cor-

rected publicly. Save your response for a quiet, private moment.

- Always give a reason for your displeasure. "Hey Jim, I really take my religious beliefs seriously, so you can imagine how I feel when you use words like 'Jesus' or 'God' so capriciously." Or, "Jim, I like to think we're all professionals here, which is probably why I find your language a little jarring."
- Recognize improvement. If your colleague cleans up his act, thank him.
- Be forgiving and reasonable. It's one thing to pepper a presentation with foul language. It's quite another to let loose when someone slams his finger in the door. Choose your openings wisely.

I admit that it's tough to correct your colleagues on this or any other indiscretion. Yet it's part of that squeeze play between faith and the marketplace. If you let this area slide, you'll find it easier to let some other, more important areas slide.

Unfortunately, the Savior's name has also become the expression of choice for many of my business associates. And what is even more distressing to me is that many men and women who consider themselves Christians have also begun using God's name in vain. I'm not sure why, but I have to admit it makes me a little sad. You don't have to swear to make it or be accepted in the business and professional worlds. I've known quite a few CEOs who did not profess Christianity, yet never used profanity. It's more an issue of self-control and common decency. So if you've developed some bad habits in this area, clean it up. Pretend your kids are listening in on your conversations. Think about the image you're portraying, and who you represent.

As a lifelong Protestant and decidedly "low church" at that, I've never put much stock in ritual or repetition. However, I have more and more been resorting to the same little ritual every time I hear the name of the Savior used in a vain or disrespectful way. Silently, I repeat this prayer: "Bless His holy name. Bless His holy name. Bless His holy name."

— —

As Christian men on our way from third to home, we will go through a lot of trash before arriving. Swearing and vulgar expressions may often impede our progress. Be ready. Know what you're going to do the next time an associate cuts loose with language that offends you. Make sure you've won the right to be heard. And when you discover your own language turning blue, get on your knees. God not only forgives, but gives you strength to throw out bad habits. Your language is often your calling card. Leave one behind that will reflect the purity and righteousness of Christ.

# How to Beat the Enemy

—  —

*But I tell you who hear me: Love your enemies, do
good to those who hate you, bless those who curse
you, pray for those who mistreat you.*

LUKE 6:27

WHEN JIM SHOWED UP for work at his new job, he expected
a little "cold shoulder" treatment from his new colleagues.
He had replaced a popular employee several years his senior, and with his Harvard MBA, Jim was naturally viewed
as an outsider. But the initial silent treatment soon became
open warfare. Proposals were met with disdain. Memos to
his boss were slanted to make Jim look bad. So Jim decided
it was time to fight fire with fire. Sharp as he was, it wasn't
difficult to expose his colleagues' motives to his boss. Two
of the culprits were fired and the others reprimanded. Soon
business was improving and everyone was rewarded for
their hard work. But Jim felt lousy about the way he had
dealt with the animosity directed at him. He had won a battle but lost the war.

—  —

Wouldn't it be nice if this scenario never happened? If
colleagues always treated you kindly and your competitors
fought fair? Unfortunately, we live in a fallen world, and
those of us in the business and professional world seem to
know it best. As Christians, there's a temptation to think

that the ethic of love and the application of noble motives do not belong in the marketplace. Too many of us preach kindness on Sunday but practice cutthroat tactics the rest of the week. In the business world, we reason, turning the other cheek will only get you slapped twice.

In my experience of televising professional sporting events, however, I've come to learn that the best way to "fight" an uncooperative foe is to employ the powerful tools of empathy, kindness, fairness, and respect. Treat even the most irascible client politely and you will soon win him over as a friend. I know. I've seen it happen over and over, and the following story is perhaps the most convincing example of how the "high road" is the right road.

The Emir, or Sheik, of Dubai became convinced that a tennis tournament would be the ideal vehicle to showcase the progress his country had made using the vast oil wealth he controlled. Never mind that there had never been a tennis tournament in Dubai, that there was no stadium, that there were no tennis officials, or that the Bedouin tribesmen who make up much of the population of Dubai would have absolutely no interest in attending a tennis tournament. The Sheik wanted a tennis tournament, so he would have a tennis tournament.

Now, a mainstay of my business is tennis tournaments. I learned a long time ago to find a few things you do well and go for it, and one thing we do well is tennis tournaments. We have organized and televised major tennis events as well as some you've never heard of. We have put together one tournament to promote European harmony (The ECC Championships in Antwerp) and another to promote capitalism (the Moscow International). So, when the Shiek wanted a tennis tournament, he called us.

With our help and his money, the Sheik built an entire tennis complex in the middle of the desert. He arranged to send one of his planes to bring in the same officials who officiated at Wimbledon to work at his event, and to import vast quantities of English strawberries and Devonshire cream. (He had heard that strawberries and cream should be served at a major tennis tournament.) Another plane ferried the players, some of the biggest names in the game, as well as the international tennis press, who were willing, even eager, to freeload at the Sheik's expense.

The Shiek also wanted his event televised, not an easy task, but one we felt we were up to. Any live sports event requiring international distribution via satellite is a fairly complex undertaking, even with a veteran crew accustomed to working together and who all speak the same language. Unfortunately, we would not have this luxury for our production in Dubai. What further complicated the task of producing four hours of television during the weekend of the Sheik's event was his mandate that several "beauty shots" be integrated with the tennis action in order to show the world Dubai's new hotels, airport, convention center, and port facilities.

Our agreement with the Sheik called for us to take only a few of our own people and to supplement the rest of the crew with staffers from Dubai Color Television, the Sheik's own network. When my partner and I went for our first meeting at Dubai Color Television, we were seated in a waiting room until the people there were ready to see us.

I began to idly pass the time by reading the waiting room literature which clearly indicated that the staff of Dubai Color Television were avid supporters of the Palestinian Liberation Organization.

Those were days when tensions were high in the Gulf. America was increasingly becoming viewed as the "Great Satan" as both Iran and the militant Arabs pumped out their messages of hate. Our little television crew from the States was seen by the Palestinians as ugly Americans—they hated us even before seeing us. Not a great way to begin a business relationship.

Our first day of meetings was a disaster. Dubai Color Television had no idea how to set up to shoot a tennis tournament or how to make arrangements to integrate the previously-produced "beauty shots" into breaks in the action. And they certainly were not about to take any suggestions, much less orders, from us. Our vital first day of on-site planning netted us nothing in the way of progress.

As our dispirited American unit met for post mortems back in the hotel, there was serious discussion about the possibility of scrapping the whole enterprise. There was also, I am ashamed to say, several disparaging remarks about "those sand niggers" with whom we needed to work. Remember, we were several thousand miles from home, forced into a working relationship with people who hated us. While I didn't condone our team's attitude, it sure was understandable. Television production is a high-stress, high-energy business and, even in the best of conditions, it is not unusual to get into shouting matches and power plays. These were not the best of conditions.

Our company had far too much riding on the event and the attendant telecasts to give it up without trying every possible way to make it work. We finally decided to try something really radical, really far out. What should have been our very first approach was tried only as a last resort. We decided to try friendship, respect, care, and understanding. Although there were Christians in our group, we had gone into the situation like hot-shot cowboys knowing we had all the answers. We had thought that if these "camel drivers" would just pay attention, we would get this thing done and be able to get out of their lousy little country. That attitude didn't work. It never does.

The next day we met our Arab colleagues with a decidedly different attitude and approach. We first made it a point to compliment them on their facilities, which included beautiful state-of-the-art equipment bought from the BBC. We then asked if we could see tapes of some of the shows they had produced, being careful to praise everything of quality in the production. This took up a whole morning, time we didn't think we had with two highly complex shoots only days away. We then surprised the Palestinians by inviting all of them back to our hotel as our guests for lunch. Some of the lower ranking technicians had never even been *inside* the Sheik's magnificent new hotel. The magic of kindness was beginning to work.

We spent the time at lunch getting to know them by name—as individuals, rather than as "that bunch of Arabs." They began showing us pictures of their families. Many were separated from wives and children by the terribly complex conflicts of the troubled region. We weren't laying cables, setting up camera positions, or running audio checks, we were doing more to insure the quality of our telecasts than anything else we could have done.

From that time on the Palestinians could not do enough for us. Because of the time we had lost due to our initial approach, we had to work far into the night during the days leading up to the event. The Palestinians were right there with us every minute, enthusiastically working long, grueling hours.

As you may have already guessed, we produced two great telecasts from the desert tennis facility marred only by Bud Collins, one of our announcers, who referred to arriving Arab dignitaries dressed in white robes as a "gaggle of geese" (nice one, Bud). In the crucible of two days of very demanding telecasts, the friendship between our crew and the Palestinians continued to grow.

The day after the event, as we stood on the tarmac of the Dubai airport waiting to board the Sheik's plane for the long flight back to London, all of the Palestinians from Dubai Color Television were there to see us off. There were many hugs. Many of the Palestinians wept openly to see the once-hated Americans leave, probably never to return. Even as our plane sat out on a far runway waiting for clearance to take off, the Palestinians waited to wave a final goodbye. As the big jet moved down the runway, we could see our new friends jumping and waving both arms over their heads, hoping to be sure we saw their final farewells. We had arrived as enemies but left as friends.

Most often in business, the temptation is to do the ignoble to gain an advantage. It is so tempting, so easy. A client forgets to return your call, so you fire off a snide FAX. A supplier sends you a wrong order so you call him up and berate him over the phone. In the desert of Dubai, we started to take the easy road but were soon forced to act nobly in order to succeed.

The real question, and one I continue to ask myself, is "Why did it take the risk of a business failure to make us act nobly toward our fellow men? Why wasn't that our first, natural approach rather than our last, calculated one?" There are many answers. None of them are pleasant. The one I think we should try to focus on is that compartmentalizing our faith, marginalizing it, always causes us to be less than God calls us to be in Christ.

Those of us on the team who were Christians were being "Sunday Christians": practicing our faith in the comfort of the sanctuary, but reverting back to our carnal selves during the work week. If we had integrated our faith into all that we did, mistakes like the one we made with the Palestinians wouldn't have happened. If our faith had really been at the center of our lives, we would have immediately seen the Palestinians as people of infinite worth because Christ died for them just as He did for us.

I recall seeing a poster once that has caused me to be more diligent in this area. It is a picture of a forlorn little child, sitting alone and sad on a dilapidated front porch of a rundown house. The caption read: "Sometimes you're the only Jesus I see." I am certain that we were the only Christians some of my Dubai Color Television colleagues had ever seen up close and personal. I hope we left a good impression.

— —

In all your business dealings, you leave a calling card. As an ambassador of Jesus Christ, your attitude on the job matters. You cannot afford to use the world's ignoble tactics, not just because it's bad for business, but because it's wrong. Today you may be tempted to fight dirty, to dress down someone who made you look bad, to slam a file on your colleague's desk and demand an answer. Don't do it. Back off and take a second look. Count to ten and pray before you act. Try to view your "opponent" as a little child waiting to see Jesus. Then respond accordingly. It will be good for business, especially the Master's.

# We All Serve Someone

—-—

*Naturally we proclaim Christ. We warn everyone we meet, teach everyone we can all that we know about Him, so that if possible we may present every man at his full maturity in Christ. This is what I am working at all the time with all the strength God gives me.*

COLOSSIANS 1:28–29 (PHILLIPS)

I HAVE THIS THING about the term "full-time Christian service." It's usually used to identify people who are paid to work in some form of a Christian organization—either a pastor, missionary, or staff member of a Christian ministry such as Youth for Christ. Even though I understand the need to make this distinction, I don't like the term. It makes it seem as if there is no alternative; that some—maybe most—Christians don't work full time for our Savior. I just don't buy that because I believe we are all called to serve Jesus at all times, whether we earn a paycheck for it or not.

Throughout my career, I have been impressed with the dedication many have to their work. Most appear to be in full-time service to their companies. I've seen cameramen who are always "on"—ready to tackle a difficult shoot, no matter what. I've watched tournament workers put in eighteen-hour days to make sure an event ran smoothly. I know these people are paid—usually very well—for their work, but I'm talking about those who go the extra mile. Those who are so sold on what they're doing that they never stop to ask about overtime or complain about being away from home.

I mention this in the context of "full-time Christian service" because I think we've let the phrase con us into thinking we can leave ministry up to the professionals. That because we don't get paid for the Christian side of our lives, we can take it kind of easy. Nothing could be farther from the truth. Whether you work with a formal ministry or as a businessman, service to God should never be an option for Christians. Perhaps the following story will illustrate the kind of dedication I believe our Lord calls us to.

During the heady days of the open tennis boom of the 1970s, one of the biggest, most glamorous and most lucrative tournaments was held in Teheran. It was the Shah of Iran's own personal event and was played at the sprawling and magnificent Imperial Country Club, the playground of the Iranian elite during the Shah's ill-fated reign.

Because the prize money was so large (the players were paid in brand new, crisp U.S. $100 bills as opposed to check or local currency), the entertainment so lavish, and first class airfare was provided, top world class professional players showed up to play. The Shah literally bought himself a tennis tournament, and his money instantly made it one of the top events in the world.

In those days, as the executive director of the Association of Tennis Professionals and the chairman of the Men's Professional Tennis Council, I was as close to being a commissioner as the sport has ever had. The manager of the Imperial Country Club, who was also director for the Shah's tournament and whose job it was to represent the event in tennis circles around the world, made it his business to build a solid friendly relationship with me.

One day on the crowded walkways of the U.S. Open at Forest Hills, the director of the Teheran tournament came up to me and said, "The Shah wants you to attend the tournament this year." Thinking it was merely a courteous gesture, I said, "Please thank his majesty for me and tell him I hope some day to visit the event." The tournament director walked away.

About five minutes later as I continued to make my way through the tennis fans at Forest Hills, the man from Teheran reappeared. Again he said, "The Shah wants you to attend the tournament this year." I was a little taken aback at this repetition but said again, "I very much appreciate the invitation. My schedule is already pretty full for that time of the year, but please express my gratitude to his majesty and tell him that one day I will come to his event." He then said, "The Shah will pay all the expenses connected with your visit." I explained that the expenses were no problem, and that I just had a different schedule for that time of the year. Again he walked away.

In about five minutes he reappeared. This time he put his hands on both my shoulders and sort of squared me up with him. He looked very directly into my eyes and said slowly and with emphasis, "The Shah wants you to attend the tournament this year." At last I got the message and said, "I'll be there." And I was.

That tournament director was executed in the earliest days of the Ayatollah's revolution in Teheran. He literally gave his life for his earthly king. When I think of his persistence with me in imparting the Shah's message, I am ashamed at how often I lack determination, consistency, and persistence in imparting the message of the King of Kings and how short I fall of Paul's work ethic described in Colossians.

Thankfully, our work never demands that kind of loyalty and dedication. But our faith does. What would happen if every Christian was as dedicated to the high calling of serving Jesus Christ? What if each Christian was as persistent with just one personal friend who has not accepted Jesus as Savior?

— —

Most of us are caught between our faith and the marketplace because we have such a compartmentalized view of life. But when you see how your faith is compatible with all that you do, the squeeze is not so tight. You can serve God through your career by living your faith each day with the kind of full-time loyalty and dedication a servant would show to his king.

# Tough Calls

—-—

*If any of you lacks wisdom, he should ask God, who gives generously to all without finding fault, and it will be given to him.*

James 1:5

HARDLY A DAY GOES by but that I have to make a decision. On a good day, the decisions are pretty easy. I usually have about three of those good days a year. The rest of the time, the decisions are tough. Real tough. In some cases, millions of dollars ride on my decisions. Make the right call, and my company makes some money. Make the wrong call, and we lose bundles.

Then there are the *real* tough ones—decisions involving people. Make the right call, and no one gets hurt. Make the wrong call, and someone's out of a job. Or worse. Those are the ones that keep me awake at night.

Fortunately, every believer has a resource to help with those decisions: the very heart and mind of God. Unfortunately, we don't always avail ourselves of this opportunity. Frankly, it sometimes seems kind of trite to go to the Lord with a decision about a business deal. He's got better things to do, we tell ourselves. And then we wonder why we're in hot water when a tough call we made goes against us.

I'll be the first to say you shouldn't be making decisions if you haven't done your homework; I don't buy the notion that you should "just hand everything over to the Lord" when it comes to making sound business decisions. God gave you brains and the ability to use them, and before you make any business decision, you had better have all the information you can humanly gather.

But we shouldn't stop there. If we take God at His word, we realize that He *does* care about the things that are important to us, and offers to guide us with His wisdom. All we have to do is ask. The following story illustrates what can happen when we forget to ask.

— —

Modern professional tennis got started during some of the most contentious days of the Cold War, and eventually got dragged into the fray. As one of the people trying to chart the course for this new, worldwide sport, I got caught in the superpowers' crossfire.

Alex Metravelli and Teimuraz Kakulia were the only two players from the Soviet Union on the professional tennis tour. They were fine players and nice guys. We became friends.

Those of us leading the sport into the professional era were determined to see that tennis be operated as openly and honestly as possible. Up to this time, under-the-table payments and a sort of seedy "shamateurism" prevailed, but we insisted that all the money made available to the players be put up in the form of prize money. Openly professional players would compete for openly announced prize money. Amateur players could also compete in the tournaments, but they only received money for their legitimate expenses and were not eligible for prize money. If an amateur wanted to compete for the money, he or she had to declare professional status.

Everyone accepted this except the Soviets. The Soviet government insisted that none of its athletes were professionals, that they were all amateurs. This was, of course, a joke. All their top athletes, including Alex and Teimuraz, were professionals. For propaganda purposes their government called them amateurs, but payed them to play.

We played along with their game and treated them like amateurs—no prize money, only expenses. But the Soviet sports authorities wanted it both ways. They wanted to maintain the dubious amateur standing of their players, and wanted the prize money they won to be sent to *them*. Not to the players, but to the Soviet sports officials. We said *nyet* to that.

I remember well the day in Paris when Metravelli came to see me to plead that exceptions be made in the rules for him and Kakulia. He told me that I could not imagine how much it meant to them to be able to travel outside the Soviet Union, and how much even the small things they were able to take back to their families helped alleviate some of the drabness of their lives. He went on to say that, unless I relented, both he and Kakulia would be ordered home and would never be allowed to compete outside the country again.

I argued that we had to make the game fair for all the players and that the rules had to be universally and impartially applied. Besides, I said, the rulers of Soviet sports would never take their two top stars off the worldwide tennis stage and forego all the great propaganda they engendered. Alex argued that, in this case, the money was much more important than the propaganda, and that if we did not relent, his and Kakulia's international tennis careers would be over. I assured him again that the Soviet bureaucrats were bluffing.

As it turned out, Alex was right and I was wrong. We enforced the rule, and I have never seen either of my Soviet friends again. They never played in another international tournament. I still hurt deeply over this.

But what hurts even more is that I never bothered to take this decision to God in prayer. I did not ask for wisdom at a time I needed it most. Instead, I barreled ahead with my own thinking and logic and ended up costing two good friends their careers.

Now, I am not suggesting that had I prayed about this tough call God would have led me to do something different. I still think I did the right thing, but I do not have that blessed assurance that comes when we commit these kinds of decisions to God. I will always be haunted by the possibility that, because I left God out of this decision, I made the wrong call and my two friends are paying the price.

I've since made about ten trips to Moscow and St. Petersburg, and each time I asked about Metravelli and Kakulia. In the Cold War days, even the tennis officials could not or would not tell me anything about them. They seemingly vanished into the vastness of that huge country. More recently, however, I met a tennis fan in St. Petersburg who knew both players, and knew Metravelli very well. She told me they had been "rehabilitated" (from what she could not say). They both were teaching tennis, Metravelli out in Soviet Georgia.

I learned the hard way from that one. I hope to meet my two friends someday and when I do, I'll ask their forgiveness—not for supporting a rule, but for not asking for God's wisdom when their careers were on the line.

Every day you make decisions, many of them involving other people, and almost all involving money. If you're like me, sometimes you wish you could just hand all the information over to someone else and let him make the call. Well, you can. God desires to impart His wisdom to you, but first you must ask. Get in the habit of praying about the tough calls you have to make at work. Lay the issues out on the table before the Lord and ask Him to direct your path. The call you make may still carry some tough consequences, but bearing them will be much easier knowing that you had the wisdom of Solomon on your side.

# Sometimes You Win,
# Sometimes You Lose

— —

*And we know that in all things God works for the good of those who love him, who have been called according to his purpose.*

Romans 8:28

THE DAY OF RECKONING has come. You did your homework, and you and your staff put together a dynamite presentation. You went before the committee and gave it your best shot. And it was a great shot. Minutes into your presentation, you knew you had them. Your graphics were superior; your facts even better. You anticipated every question and answered it before it could even be asked. You could almost hear cheers as you sat down, and now the call is coming through with the results.

"You guys did a great job, Bob, but we've decided to go with XYZ."

— —

"You win some, you lose some, and some get rained out." This old philosophical approach to baseball is, perhaps, a useful way for most of us to view our lives in the business and professional world. Unless your job is making widgets on a machine that knocks out a perfect little widget every time, you will certainly have your ups and down, your wins and losses, your rainouts. That's business. That's life.

In the strange, arcane world of television, I have had many more losses than wins. In this business, only about one idea in a hundred ever ends up as a program people actually see on their TV sets. For my few successes, I've had hundreds of rejections. Hundreds of carefully planned, time- and money-consuming presentations that have made it to almost the final clearance only to be shot down.

Fortunately, the one idea in a hundred that is successful produces an exhilarating high. It's a definite kick to turn on your TV set and see something that a year or so ago was only an idea, a vision in your mind, and be able to see it jump off the screen, available for millions of people to see. Winning awards for those ideas, which my company has been fortunate enough to do, makes it even better. Those are the things that keep me going.

My hunch is that in your business or profession, you also have a lot of highs and lows—and probably more lows than highs. The challenge for Christians is to keep our business successes and failures in perspective. If success becomes the end all, then the resulting fear of failure may drive us to do things we otherwise wouldn't do.

The Bible clearly teaches that we should have a special feeling for and commitment to our work. We are to strive for excellence in all we do, to provide for our families, and to take satisfaction in a job well done. But while our work is important, it only partially defines who we are. Too often, we seek our complete identity through what we do for a living. This can set us up to become slaves to success and cause us to handle failures badly. I believe God expects us to do our best and then hand the results—the wins *and* the losses—over to Him.

The toughest type of failures to handle is that which comes despite the fact that you deserved to win. Several years ago our little company had a chance to grab a great promotion and distribution contract for Major League Baseball. Everything was working in our favor. My partner had been a classmate at Yale with the baseball commissioner. We had key executives with a vast knowledge of baseball. We had experience in international baseball production and we had more than twenty years of international television sales with the NBA. Going into the final presentation, we had a virtual lock on the contract, but we still approached our time before the commissioner as if we were the underdog. In other words, we put together a final presentation that was first class. Everything seemed to work. Everything felt right.

I still remember almost every word of the call when it came. Fay Vincent, then the deputy commissioner to the late Bart Giamatti, made the call: "You guys made the best presentation and went to the top of the list." Then came the most dreaded word in the English language: "But," Fay continued, "we are giving the job to NBC."

I couldn't believe what I was hearing. NBC is a great network but they had made only a perfunctory effort to get this international distribution contract. They had acted as if they didn't even want it. But when word had gotten back to the brass at General Electric, NBC's parent company, of the poor impression that was made, orders came down for them to go back and get the deal no matter what it took. They were in, we were out.

Now that hurt big-time, but I was able to handle the loss because I knew we had done our best and that there was more to life than a big contract. I handed over disappointment to God and walked away. I had no idea why He allowed this to happen in my life, but I trusted Him.

We lost that contract through no fault of our own, but believe me, I've lost other deals due to my own stupidity. And I'm here to tell you that God is with you through those trials as well. Let me give you an example. For many years we've been going out to Asia for sales jaunts that often include cities like Kuala Lumpur, Singapore, Beijing, and Jakarta. It's a tough, grueling schedule that we informally and privately refer to as the "Bataan Death March." At a dinner one evening with a Japanese man and his wife who ran a major company in Japan, I used that phrase. Goodbye deal. Goodbye friendship. You can believe I now make it a practice to never use any kind of slang expression when associating with foreign clients, thanks to my "Bataan Death March" remark.

I'm sure you've never done anything that stupid, but you've probably made a few blunders that cost you or your company some big dollars. While I do not suggest you become lackadaisical about your performance, it is important to keep an eternal perspective on these kinds of mistakes. You are not perfect, but you do serve a perfect God who wants you to be the very best for His sake. Rather than beat yourself up over your errors, learn from them.

By the way, very shortly after getting overlooked by Major League Baseball, God showed us he had a better, more important baseball assignment for us. He brought the former San Francisco Giants' pitcher, Dave Dravecky, across our path. Dave's story is one of commitment to Christ in spite of suffering and circumstance. When I met him he was looking for a way to use television to broaden the impact of the message and witness he had shared through his books. Isn't that just like God? I lost a huge contract to distribute baseball programming around the globe, but got the chance to produce "Dravecky: A Story of Courage and Grace," a one-hour long documentary that has already been seen by millions. For me, it is infinitely more satisfying to have "won" a part of the Dravecky project than to have distributed a thousand baseball games to networks around the world.

—  —

God not only minimizes your losses, He makes them work for you. But first, you need to put your career in the proper perspective. Is it something you are selfishly pursuing for your own fame or material gain? Or is it a labor of love that you willingly give to God? How you answer that question makes a big difference in how you handle those losses that inevitably come around.

# A Final Word

— —

*Forgetting what is behind and straining toward what is ahead, I press on toward the goal to win the prize for which God has called me heavenward in Christ Jesus.*

PHILIPPIANS 3:13–14

THIS BOOK HAS BEEN about the tight squeeze we sometimes feel between our faith and the work world. I would like to close with a story that both humbles me, yet encourages me to do a better job of being salt and light in the world.

In my years of working at the higher echelons of professional sports and television, I've had the privilege of working with some of the greatest sports writers in the business. Guys like Jim Murray, the Pulitzer Prize winning sports columnist of the *Los Angeles Times*, Edwin Pope, the highly lauded sports star of the *Miami Herald*, and Blackie Sherrod, the "Sage of the Southwest, who continues to bring his insightful attention to bear on college football for the *Dallas Morning News*.

Since I've spent the major portion of my career in professional tennis, it is no accident that I've developed a relationship with perhaps the greatest tennis writer in the world, Rex Bellamy of the *Times of London*. The *Times*, almost the paper of record for the sport worldwide, assigned Rex to the tennis beat in the early sixties, and he covered it like no one else through parts of four decades. Rex amazed his readers, his editors, his sports writing peers, and tennis insiders with the beauty of his writing, the sagacity of his insights, and the fearlessness of his convictions.

When I came into tennis in 1967, Rex was the voice of the game, the best writer on the most influential paper. Both because it was an important part of my job to be acquainted with the top writer in the sport, and because I genuinely admire good writing, I began to build a relationship with Rex.

Keep in mind that it's highly unusual for a sports writer to have a close personal relationship with a person who is part of the sport he is covering. Even in the best of circumstances there is something of an adversarial relationship. Conflict is inherent in most relationships between writer and subject, so for a friendship to blossom beyond the purely professional level is very rare indeed.

All that notwithstanding, almost from the start Rex and I began to build a solid, most enjoyable, and treasured friendship. Don't get me wrong; our friendship certainly did not keep us from tangling professionally. I had my tennis agenda, and he had his. When he thought my agenda was not in the best interest of the sport, he said so very powerfully in the *Times* and other important tennis publications. Needless to say, this made my job difficult—sometimes even impossible, it seemed.

In spite of frequent disagreements, Rex's demeanor toward me personally was always warm and cordial. He could disagree very forcefully with my vision for the sport, but be very supportive of me personally. In one treasured article in the *Times* Rex wrote, ". . . Briner is a man to be trusted," while in that same article he questioned a decision I had made.

What a lesson for Christians who sometimes find it difficult to disagree and yet remain friends. I think of the many divisions within the church that come from not being able to separate the professional from the personal, and it grieves me. But that's not the point of my story.

As our friendship grew, we brought our wives into the circle. We visited each other's homes. We ate together whenever we could, wherever we could. During our many times together, Rex and I found plenty to talk about beyond tennis. In addition to being a world-class authority on the sport, Rex wrote several books on England's national parks and the many hiking and camping opportunities they afford. We talked often about this, and about business, art, television, international politics, food, and any other number of topics which arise freely when two men who like each other get together. But for some reason, we never once talked about spiritual matters, issues of faith and religion. I don't recall deliberately avoiding the subject; it just never came up.

I met Rex Bellamy in 1967. It was not until 1993, when I read a review he had written for his church publication of *Roaring Lambs*, that I had any indication of Rex's interest in the things of God. Until he read my book, he had no indication of my interest in and commitment to Christ and His Kingdom. Talk about being ashamed!

After I read his review, I made one of the sheepiest transatlantic phone calls I have ever made. I had been just about the opposite of the "roaring lamb" I had tried to write about. For twenty-six years, I had kept my faith a virtual secret from a much respected friend and colleague. To his credit, Rex was just about as sheepish as I was when I reached him at his home in the English countryside.

Consider the rich spiritual fellowship we missed during those twenty-six years. Think of all we could have learned from each other. Think of the kind of witness we might have provided had we been emboldened to act together in His cause.

As you might guess, I have spent a lot of uncomfortable time thinking about all those years of spiritual silence within the bounds of a lively, dynamic, and enjoyable friendship. Why did it happen that way? Why was I so timid about my faith?

Many answers have come hurtling back to me—none very flattering, and none that can be used as an excuse. The only conclusion I can draw is one that pertains to a problem which has plagued my spiritual life so often and which I am certain plagues so many others: compartmentalization. I kept God in the church on Sunday or in my devotions in a hotel room and left Him there. I did not see why or how He could be a part of my business and professional life. The result was the kind of debilitating and shameful situation that I experienced with Rex.

━ ━

When we fail to live a fully integrated life—one in which our faith impacts all we do—we rob ourselves and others of the joy of a Christ-centered life. We keep unbelievers from coming in contact with the Gospel. Don't let the same thing happen to you. Constantly seek an integrated life. Be vigilant to see that your faith relates positively to all you do. Be certain that your business and professional friends know who you really are and *whose* you really are.

Every day you may find yourself caught between the blessings of your faith and the demands of your career. You have enough stress at work and don't need the additional stress of this "squeeze play." The only way out of it is to put your faith in Christ first. Even before you cross the plate, the only Umpire who really counts has already signaled an irrevocable hands-down "safe" call. You don't have to be hung up between third and home. That base path ought to be a cake walk because we know the Holy Spirit will take us safely home.

So live joyfully with eternity in mind. Honor God by believing His promises. Inspire others by exuding God's peace and serenity. And someday soon, I look forward to a great postgame press conference where we can all join the Savior in a marvelous, never-ending celebration!